OVERCOMING THE FEAR OF DEATH AND DYING

A Sense of Life That Knows No Death

JESS E. WEISS

Brookville Books
Old Brookville, NY

Also by Jess E. Weiss

THE VESTIBULE
THE ADAM AND EVE FANTASY
A CONVERSATION WITH GOD

I am not Omar Khayyam,
I am that I am
For better or worse.

So don't be glad
And don't be sad,
Simply ReJoyce.

Jess E. Weiss

Acknowledgments

To: Andrew Sinclair and Gertrude Stenquist Sinclair of Waltham, Massachusetts; Carl J. and Philadelphia Welz of Carmel Valley, California; Robert Dolling Wells and Rev. Ralph Mero, M.Div., of Seattle Washington; Rev. George F. Dole of Sharon, Massachusetts; Professor J. Theodore Klein of Newton, Massachusetts; Harry Costello of Northport, Long Island, New York; Shamim Ahmed of Oyster Bay Cove, New York; Rolf Witzsche of North Vancouver, BC, Canada—as a token of my appreciation for their kind interest in this book. *And to:* Marilyn Fenton of Amherst, New Hampshire, whose editing brought the substance of this subject into greater focus.

OVERCOMING THE FEAR OF DEATH AND DYING
A Sense of Life That Knows No Death

Library of Congress Catalog Card Number: 91-76378

ISBN: 0-87957-014-8

Published by Brookville Books, 333 Glen Head Road, Old Brookville, NY 11545

Copyeditor: Maureen Sullivan Drury
Cover design: Jeff Thurau

Printed and bound in the United States of America.

THE MOTH

I had just finished this book; it was in the computer awaiting the print-out tap, when the need for a stretch and a breath of air prompted me to go out. It was a still, warm evening, when the late-setting sun sets my back-yard aglow. At the slope of our steep little hill leading to the rear of our house are seven steps. To the left of the steps are a bird bath and a drinking fountain. As I walked past the bird bath, I observed a large ephemeral moth that had fallen in and was struggling frantically to stay afloat and escape the gravity suction of the water. For a moment I watched its vain attempt to free itself and then started to pass it by. "It's only a common moth," I thought, when a voice I wasn't certain was mine cried, "Help me." I took a closer look and thought, "I'm alive and so is this fragile, short-lived creature. I don't particularly like or dislike moths, but I assume that, like myself, a moth has a purpose in this world or it would not be here. What that purpose is I don't really know, but do I need to know? We, that moth and I, share this place, this moment, and life itself." Instantly I swooped it up, and it flew into the luminous evening air. For that tiny moment I felt a sense of being at one with something greater than myself.

A young man said to a very old man,
''What is your greatest worry as you grow old?''
The elder replied,
''My greatest concern is that THIS is all there is to life.''
Jess E. Weiss

I dedicate this book
to those who envision man as Eternal,
and therefore ageless.

And deliver them who through
fear of death were all their
lifetime subject to bondage.
Hebrews 2:15 KJV

Contents

Foreword

I WAS DELIGHTED to receive a working copy of Jess Weiss's *Overcoming the Fear of Death and Dying: A Sense of Life That Knows No Death*. This masterful book confirmed my life, my experience, my feelings about the living process. Yes, we can have it all: beauty, power, vitality and zest into our later years. We can actually pass on into another reality not having totally destroyed our bodies and minds by "outdated philosophies and beliefs" about the maturing process. It *is* a process, and all processes have inherent within them a way of living which allow us to take full advantage of every year of our lives.

We live the way we think.
We live the way we feel.
We mature the way we envision.

Overcoming the Fear of Death and Dying: A Sense of Life That Knows No Death provides one of the best support systems for living totally, always, throughout our lives. Jess Weiss is a maverick. He is an irritation to the tired way of living that has taken over so many people. He is an example of a truth that works: we can leave this planet in our later latter years fully conscious, fully productive and fully active. It is a matter of truly wanting this type of passage.

It is a matter of saying "yes" to each minute of each day. It is a matter of "kicking the heck out of each day!" *It is about the courage to be! Always!*

What factors work together to keep us young, alert, active and vigorous? What beliefs, convictions, attitudes and emotions contribute to successful agelessness? How does our keeping young spiritually and mentally influence the body's renewal process? How can we achieve happiness, health, and vitality at any time of life, even in our present circumstances?

All these questions are so beautifully explored in *Overcoming the Fear of Death and Dying: A Sense of Life That Knows No Death* that I sat at the edge of my reading chair as I totally immersed myself in this enthralling and revealing book. Jess Weiss is a "kick in the pants." He knows how to live fully; he has mastered the joy and richness that is possible, and he frankly passes them on to his readers. He has hit the mark that explodes our false beliefs about aging and sees the many possibilities that are available to the human race for living totally "alive" throughout our entire lives. Pass this book on to your young ones after you've read it—it is best to develop this bright way of living very early in life!

Overcoming the Fear of Death and Dying: A Sense of Life That Knows No Death presents a most impressive possibility. It is an open sharing of what life can really rise to. It takes the concept of "over the hill" and completely demolishes it. It blows away the assumption that senility and old-age sickness are inevitable. It erases the worn-out belief that we must live the short, sickly lifespans of our forebears. The translating of positive ideas into constructive action is the essence of living always in a young manner, always, and the method available to each of us who truly desires to play all out. Jess Weiss knows the truth of his writing. He has tested his beliefs and his philosophies, and they are no longer just beliefs but facts. By the time I completed reading this book, I had entirely, again, changed my concept of aging, renewal, and perpetual youth. Later years need not bring deterioration in either the physical or mental ability of senior adults. Research is constantly pointing out that health, activity, and productivity in the mature years are determined to a great extent by the choices we make about beliefs, habitual thought patterns, and early lifestyle. Much of the decline once believed to be caused by aging is actually the result of harmful habits of thinking or action—habits that can be corrected so that healing and renewal of mind and body may occur.

In short, this book boldly states that our calendar years in no way can measure our spirit, ideas, or understanding of who and what we truly are: *Vital sources of aliveness —always.*

I want to openly thank Jess Weiss for his contribution to a richer, fuller life for myself. Again another "new age thinker" has shed great light on the immense possibilities that are available to each of us living youthfully late in life with a sense of existence that knows no death.

Robert Pante
Author and Lecturer,
Kailua, Hawaii

Jess Weiss cuts through a great deal of nonsense about aging and dying, and he does so with energy, humor, and the full wisdom of his years. If you find pleasure in self-pity, steer clear.

Rev. George F. Dole, Ph.D.
Swedenborg School of Religion

Preface

MY BOOK *The Vestibule* was published in 1972 and is still in print, comforting patients and their families in hospices and similar settings for the terminally ill. In it I sought to answer the question, "Is there life after death?" I was one of the first to publish documentary experiences of those who died and returned to share their "death experiences" with us. Those who had the "near death" and "out-of-body" experiences, gave similar testimonies:

> *They felt no pain or suffering during the experience. In fact, they recalled a feeling of tranquillity and peace. They had a panoramic view of their entire lives. They felt the presence of loved ones who had died earlier. They were in the presence of an undefined radiant Light. They went through a tunnel and upon their return to human life-form, death was no longer an enemy to fear. They were very certain, afterwards, that life goes on without interruption after the body dies.*

Death awaits us all, and no matter what we may do, or how we may live, we cannot deliver ourselves from that death on our own initiative. Unless something greater than ourselves can revive us from death, we have no hope beyond the grave.

It was the similarity of the out-of-body narratives that made me realize that consciousness and body can exist separately, that consciousness is not bound by the body. I became aware that I am not simply inside my body looking out. Death is rather a transition from time and space, a reentry into eternity; and as man was created in the image of God originally, he is therefore also the image of God eternally. The researching and writing of that book twenty years ago enables me today to understand the effect that aging and dying has on the man or woman who knows that life is infinite and eternal, as opposed to the one who doubts or remains ignorant. It provides the basis for this current endeavor. I do not know a way around the aging and dying process—but I do know a comforting, procrastinating, and inspirational way through it.

Overcoming the Fear of Death and Dying is a nondenominational, ecumenical, metaphysical and mystical approach to long life in the ideal. It speaks to a broad audience of earnest readers who ask, "What about the latter years?" The inspirational writings in this book counteract the interpretation of mortality as reality. They express my way of worshipping God and of transcending consciously, even if momentarily, to an eternal sense of existence. Such writings have been an elixir and an extension of my inner Self. They have made my human sense of life bearable under the most difficult of circumstances. How impoverished life would seem were I unable to think and write on such transcendental subjects! My life would be empty, and my human existence would have no real significance.

Jess E. Weiss

Introduction

. . . my lifetime is as nothing in thy sight.
Psalm 39:5 RSV

WE MODERN men and woman of the Western World have cultivated an insatiable desire for long life. At the same time we harbor deep-rooted fear of what we call "old age." Our culture encourages a mania to stay physically fit and youthful in appearance. And modern medicine progresses, buoying our hopes. Stay alive, we tell ourselves, no matter how, no matter what the circumstance; human life is all we have, and life under any circumstance is preferable to fearful, inevitable death.

There are physicians who cater to our fears, who want to keep us alive under any conditions. Longevity rather than good quality of life becomes paramount. Such doctors are intent on prolonging our lives and reanimating our bodies through the implantation of artificial hearts or the transplantation of a kidney, heart, liver or lung from a deceased body to a living body. Organ harvesting, cloning and cryonics may fast become signs of our times. Modern advances have embroiled us in the moral dilemma of deciding who lives and how, and who dies so another can live. And we often consent to medical experimentation as a way of increasing longevity. But shouldn't the primary goal, the central objective of modern medicine, be the improvement of life's *quality* rather than simply its extension? To cure rather than to just take care? A long life is not necessarily a better life.

Hippocrates, the father of medicine, lived four centuries before Jesus Christ, when the average lifespan was thirty years, and few people lived long enough to suffer old-age afflictions. The obligation of physicians under the Hippocratic Oath should be redefined to contend with the moral complexities of modern medical practice. Scientific advancements will allow the terminally ill to live longer, but fewer of them may want to live when they comprehend that it means a body attached interminably to a machine. Such a vision is truly the terrifying specter of our age. Prolonging a life of incurable agony in which a body is curled up in a fetal ball, tethered to a life-support system, pain and hopelessness: dehumanization. These turn the ethics of medicine upside down.

In addition, there is a bitter debate between those who believe that people should be allowed to die with dignity and those who argue that even life in a vegetative, incontinent state has meaning. The latter would deprive us of our autonomy and of our ability to take care of our own bodies. It has become necessary to invent legal directives to protect a patient who wishes life-extension treatment to cease. The Right To Die movement in this country has responded by stressing quality of life in preference to the tendency of modern hospitals and doctors to want to thwart the "last enemy." Most of us have the desire to live as long as we are mentally in control of our bodies. But at precisely the moment we might want to die, we may lose the capacity to make that choice. We want to be sure we are extending life, and not death.

Today's physicians have the ability, based on advanced technology, to keep a patient alive almost indefinitely. But for what? What do terminally-ill patients do in an age of medical technology and self-congratulation?

Either the right to live and the right to die are both sacred, or neither is. In November, 1991, a new federal patients-rights bill quietly became law. As a sort of medical "Miranda" warning, the law requires hospitals, nursing homes, health maintenance organizations and hospices to acquaint patients in writing with legal options for refusing or accepting life support and other medical treatment if they become incapacitated. The federal law creates no new rights, only choices about the right to say "Enough." New York State has a health-care proxy law. Under this law, competent adults can execute a simple document naming anyone they choose to act as their proxy in making decisions, should they become unable to act on their own behalf. And, there is a movement slowly building within the health-care system to concentrate less on technologies that prolong dying, and more on making natural death more comfortable. A group of doctors calling themselves Physicians for Death With Dignity has formed to encourage other physicians to 'come out of the closet' on physician-assisted death. Extension of life is important, but surely a person's essence, one's existence beyond today and tomorrow, should be a part of the picture. The purpose of this book is not to be without compassion about birth, age and dying, but to lift them higher through spiritualization of thought—an attempt to separate the tares from the wheat. Human age is not the substance (understanding) of Eternal-life. Let's then try to step back, to step out of time and space, and loosen the mental constraints by which we contemplate this life. If we analyze our problem differently, from not only the physical, but also the metaphysical and spiritual point of view, then this transient human body can be recognized as simply a mortal vehicle, not a person's ultimate "truth." One can *know* the truth about the body, but one cannot *create* the truth. The human body is an incredible, miraculous mechanism, but it is still, after all, just a temporary fleshly house with a conscious tenant. And age is not a span of years, but a progressive unfolding of everlasting life. Some of us see and feel only limitation as the body ages. Others, with discernment and perspicacity, feel only possibilities. Is the cup that is my life half full or half empty? We cannot overcome age by embracing youth, but we can train our thought consciously and continuously to go into new paths, dwelling neither on the past nor the future.

Each human being has two identities: one visible, the other invisible; one tangible, the other intangible; one mortal, the other immortal; one finite, the other infinite; one enlightened, the other unenlightened; one which lives in earth-consciousness, the other in God-consciousness. God-consciousness really means understanding that Eternity is omnipresent *now, without past, present or future.* And God-consciousness never returns to dust. Man is God's infinite offspring. The human psyche is a symposium of good and evil thoughts and it is often a consciousness divided against itself. "A double minded man is unstable in all his ways," said the author of the epistle of St. James (1:8 KJV). In reality there is but one "image and likeness" of God, and that is the undivided human being whose primary devotion to God lets God dwell in that person. We must increase our faith in the usefulness, wisdom, and vigor of our advancing years and reject any expectation of decrepitude and debility. Loss of vitality and ability is inconsistent when we view our lives in the light of His image and likeness. All too often when we grasp our mutable, finite sense of life with the left hand, we unknowingly let go of an immutable, infinite, endless, and ageless sense of life with the right hand. William Shakespeare's Hamlet said: "What a piece of work is man; how noble in reason; how infinite in faculty. . . in apprehension how like a God."

> *I have no pleasure in the death of him that dieth, said the Lord God: wherefore turn yourselves, and live.*
>
> Ezekiel 18:32 KJV

Age is a decoy, a human invention of a beginning and an ending, a misconception which imposes boundaries for life, and we give it the only life it has. We then allow ourselves to become the victims of our own creation, prisoners of a calendar of time and numbers, birth and death, and of the belief that life on this uncertain plane of existence is measured by the revolutions of the earth around the sun. We need to be led out of this self-imposed bondage. Death out of season is a mistake. The timely death of a body is simply time for renewal. As bodily creatures we exist in nature, yet we are able to transcend nature. By developing a transcendental vision about our bodies, we also transcend that material concept in which we are so deeply rooted and falsely educated. It is our misuse, distortion, and perversion of our bodies that causes them to suffer, to age unnecessarily and to die prematurely. But human life is infinitely beyond the fleeting phases of aging mortality. Longevity is earth-time, immortality endless-time.

The outer life earth
Is man's finite mortality,
The earthly concept of reality.
The Eternal inner life
Is man's infinite immortality,
The awakened Christ reality.

Jess E. Weiss

"Be still and know that I am God" (Psalm 46:10 KJV). By stilling the turbulence of thoughts and the restlessness of the finite body, and by allowing ourselves to be transformed by the renewing of the mind, we begin to sense the infinite "I am" of being, the agelessness of perpetual existence that is now and has always been here and now.

Be not ignorant of this one thing,
that one day is with the Lord as a
thousand years, and a thousand years
as one day.

2 Peter 3:8 KJV

Part I

If you look at yourself and are aware of what is really there, you will not see either youth or age but man, the Eternal child of God.

Robert Dolling Wells
The Network Newsletter

Chapter I

How Old Is Old?

I NEVER KNEW my mother's age until I was required to submit her death certificate to the proper authorities after she died, and I intend to honor her secret. She seemed to have found the mythical fountain of youth, and she appeared twenty years younger than her attained age. A natural brunette, sans grey hair, she had a baby-like complexion with not a wrinkle, and a set of naturally white teeth that sparkled all the time because she smiled all the time. The real beauty was hidden in the nature of the woman. Always vibrant, compassionate, interested in others, sympathetic and helpful, she had a zest for living that helped her through the vicissitudes of human life. Often she was mistaken for my sister, not because I looked older than my age, but because she looked years younger than hers and acted the part naturally. "You can't help getting older, but you don't have to get old." This was her belief and practice.

Whether young or old, age touches us all. Recently I said to my father-in-law, an energetic, feisty "fire ball" going on 89, "Father, close your eyes and tell me how old you really are right now." "Twenty-four going on thirty-four," and as his eyes opened, he concluded, "Youth is a feeling and an attitude, not numbers." It is a paradox that very young people look forward to getting older, and when they become older, they want to slow the process down, and even reverse it. We are not responsible for being forty, sixty, or eighty or more years of age—it happens to the best of us if we live long enough—but we are individually responsible for being and acting old at any age.

> There is no definition for "old" except attitude and mobility. Attitude tells whether you are old or not. If you are curious, challenging, doing something, you are not old.
>
> Art Linkletter, at 78

We are accustomed to seeing things get old. To this world everything appears to have a beginning, a period of usefulness, and an end. We mark this progression of events on our clocks, our diaries, our calendars. We define reality by our five physical senses and measure it in hours, days, and years. We understand only progression from birth to babyhood, to childhood, to adolescence, to adulthood, to middle age, and to old age and death. "Age is unnecessary," said Shakespeare's King Lear. I think that Shakespeare meant that one's belief in time, in the calendar, is the hidden subconscious mathematician of age.

Scientists are not sure exactly why we age. Some have thought we are biologically and genetically programmed to age, yet to others age is just an infinitesimal part of eternity. What then is old age? Is it merely a state of mind? Is it the result of physical and emotional events manifesting themselves in one's appearance? Does it have anything to do with numbers? Margaret Chase Smith, Maine's former Republican senator, celebrating her ninetieth birthday, said, "I think of myself as seventy. I've never really thought of age in terms of years. I've seen so many people who were old at forty, or young at eighty." Could it perhaps be that old age is that stage or numbered age in a person's life when he or she has become bored with himself and with his concept of the world?

In the little village of Kutol, hidden away in the foothills of the Caucasus Mountains at the southern tip of the U.S.S.R., live some of the world's oldest people. Here is what they told *National Geographic* magazine (January 1973) regarding their longevity:

> When asked what age he thought youth extends to, Gabriel Chapnian, age 117, replied, "Youth normally extends up to age 80. I was still young then." When asked his prescription for longevity, he concluded with a twinkle in his eye, "Active physical work and a moderate interest in alcohol and the ladies." Quada Jonashian, aged 110, thought "youth" meant engaging in sexual activity and admitted that he had considered himself a "youth" up until "a dozen years ago." Miguel Carpio, a 123-year-old patriarch stated, "I would not like to be young again, but if I could just take 15 years from my age, wonderful! Oh, to be 108 again!"

The *1990 Guiness Book of World Records* tells us that the greatest authenticated age to which any human has ever lived is a unique 120 years 237 days in the case of Shigechiyo Izumi of Japan. He was born June 29, 1865, and recorded as a six-year-old in Japan's first census of 1871; he died February 21, 1986. The oldest living person in the world whose date of birth can be reliably authenticated is Carrie C. White of Palatka, Florida, who was born November 18, 1874. (Died February, 1991.)

Our preoccupation with our common problem, "age," is obvious, and each of us comes to terms with it in our own way, often with an element of macabre humor. Witticisms about the elderly are found displayed on the bumper stickers of automobiles: "Semi-retired, Semi-impossible," "Happiness is being a grandparent," "Live long, get revenge, be a burden to your children," "I'm not getting older, just better." A humorist quipped, "What is old age? Old age is wisdom, patience, understanding, and irregularity." Other observations and definitions communicate the attitudes of pessimists and optimists..

The Pessimists (who are people who view themselves as optimists with experience):

''Due to circumstances beyond my control, I may live too long.''
''Aging is a time of diminished status rather than of fulfillment.''
''I never planned for old age.''
''If I knew I was going to live this long,
I would have taken better care of myself.''
''I'm not dead, I just got tired of living.''
''I'm one of the over-the-hill gang, 40-plus.''

To them "Old Age" is. . .

When you get winded playing chess.
When your children begin to look middle-aged.
When you sink your teeth into a steak and they stay there.
When your back goes out more than you do.
When you look forward to a dull evening.
When dialing long distance wears you out.

When your little black book has only names ending in M.D.
When what you used to do all night, now takes all night to do.

The Optimists have a different view.

Wrinkles merely indicate where smiles have been.
''If you should survive to 105, think of all you'll derive out of being alive.''
''Old age is not something I've stayed off; it's something I've achieved. I'm having a ball,'' Helen Hayes, actress, at 88.
''On the whole, I'd rather be in Philadelphia,'' W.C. Field's own epitaph.
When death knocks on the door, I don't answer; I'm not in.
''I don't intend to die; there's no future in it,'' George Burns at 94.
''I'm not afraid to die; I just don't want to be there when it happens,'' Woody Allen.
''I cannot hold back the numbers, but I don't have to count,'' Martha Weiss, birth-date unknown.
''Johnston is my name and forever young is my game.''
''Grow old along with me, the best is yet to be.''
When I die, at least I'll get rid of my allergies.
And my own philosophy: ''If I gotta die, let me die young, very late in life.''

We live in a society that places a tremendous emphasis on youth and fixation on age. When young schoolchildren were asked "What is aging?" they replied, "Getting old," "Having false teeth and gray hair," "Getting wrinkles," "Getting sick," "Being in the hospital all the time," "Sitting in a wheelchair waiting to die," "Dying," "Going to funerals," "Going to the cemetery." In other words, being old is all the things that being young is not.

Aging has been described as a decline from a peak of youth. When asked to define "old age," people under thirty said sixty-three was old, people between thirty and thirty-nine said sixty-seven was old, people forty to forty-nine said seventy was old, people fifty to fifty-nine said seventy-one was old, people sixty to sixty-four said seventy-three was old, and people older than sixty-five said seventy-five was old. Somewhere between the ages of thirty and forty, however, one's thoughts become subtly or subliminally centered upon what one thinks he or she has lost, that is, the prime of youth. So when is a person in his or her prime, and exactly what is prime? What is old, and when is a person considered to be old? Who sets the norm? The answer is that mentally, arithmetically, it is *we* who label ourselves young or old, and then we act the part. It could be diagnosed as self-malpractice. I submit that young or old is not the heart's desire: graceful maturity is, whatever the age. We actually have two ages: our chronological age and our functional age. According to Ken Dychtwald, in *Wellness and Health Promotion for the Elderly* (Aspen, 1986): "Tomorrow's elderly will have traveled to more places, will have read more books and magazines, will have met more people, will have lived longer, and will be part of a more powerful 'elderculture' than any previous cohort in the history of the world." Old age is in the eye and mind of the beholder. Age does not reside in a physical body, but is self-imposed, a focused thought, a mental acceptance. The physical body is always and in all ways the obedient servant of the human mentality.

We have all heard someone told, "Act your age." And why, indeed, should anyone "act one's age?" There exists today an Atlantic City-based beauty pageant in which contestants must be at least sixty years old. Judges base their decision on interview, evening gown, talent and, most of all, philosophy of life. Ms. Senior America 1990 is just sixty-eight years of age. When asked to outline the "five action words" that guided her life, she replied: "looking, listening, learning, loving and living life with the expectation of the very best." This year a new magazine entitled, *Longevity,* hit the newsstands. Its credo: "Throw the words 'old age' out the window." There is also a National Senior Sports Association (NSSA), a membership organization which sponsors senior golf, tennis and bowling tournaments at resorts around the country. Want to join the competition? Try the National Golf Foundation, the National Bowling Council, the National Association of Senior Citizens Softball, the 70+ Ski Club, or the U.S. National Senior Olympics. "I am now convinced that the emotional benefits are greater than the physical benefits," said Lloyd Wright, the founder of the NSSA.

Sport knows no age limit. A Boston research team wrote recently in the *Journal of the American Medical Association* of interesting results seen in nine nursing home residents beyond age ninety, who participated in a weight-training program. Eight weeks of high-intensity weight-lifting led to muscle increases of as much as 174 percent, thigh muscle size increases of about 9 percent and walking speed increases of 48 percent. The report concluded that "high-resistance weight training leads to significant gains in muscle strength, size and functional mobility among frail residents of nursing homes up to ninety-six years of age." We don't stop playing and exercising because we are old, we are old because we stopped playing and exercising.

What then does "normal aging" mean? Hulda Crooks, who in July 1987, at the age of ninety-one, climbed 12,388 feet to the summit of Mount Fuji, Japan's highest mountain, said, "You must have a goal to survive." Jacques-Yves Cousteau, preparing to re-embark on an ambitious around-the-world excursion in his famous ship "Calypso," regarding his age (79) remarked: "As long as I'm in good health, I feel as if I'm 50. Why should I stop? The world is big and a lifetime is nothing." Margaret Lambert of Dillon, Colorado, this year won three gold medals in cycling track (800 meters) and one in walking (1,500 meters) in the Senior Olympics. At the Rocky Mountain Senior Winter Games she won four golds in skiing and added a fifth in speed skating. She is 67. Dr. Paul Spangler, a 91-year-old retired naval surgeon, who has medals in masters competition around the country, competed in the 1990 New York City Marathon. In preparing for this major event he logged 25-30 miles per week, including long runs of 15-20 miles a day. He said prior to the race, "I have a new mantra for my meditation. I'm going to repeat it to myself throughout the race: 'I know I can.' And when I finish, it's going to be: 'I knew I could.'" And he did. This concept recalls the philosophy of Horace Kallen, who said: "There are persons who shape their lives by the fear of death, and there are persons who shape their lives by the joy of life. The former live, dying; the latter die living. When I die, I intend to die living."

Youth

Youth is not a time of life; it is a state of mind; it is not a matter of rosy cheeks, red lips and supple knees; it is a matter of the will, a quality of the imagination, a vigor of the emotions; it is the freshness of the deep springs of life.

Youth means a temperamental predominance of courage over timidity, of the appetite for adventure over the love of ease. This often exists in a man of 60 more than a boy of 20. Nobody grows old merely by a number of years. We grow old by deserting our ideals.

Years may wrinkle the skin, but to give up enthusiasm wrinkles the soul. Worry, fear, self-distrust bows the heart and turns the spirit back to dust.

Whether sixty or sixteen, there is in every human being's heart the lure of wonder, the unfailing child-like appetite of what's next, and the joy of the game of living. In the center of your heart and my heart there is a wireless station: so long as it receives messages of beauty, hope, cheer, courage and power from men and from the Infinite, so long are you young.

When the aerials are down, and your spirit is covered with snows of cynicism and the ice of pessimism, then you are grown old, even at 20; but as long as your aerials are up, to catch waves of optimism, there is hope you may die young at 80.

Readers Digest 1990

Act your age.
The one has nothing to do with the other.

Chapter II

Living by the Numbers

I WISH I could tell you that if we live right, we will live indefinitely; but all human beings have one thing in common, however prudently we live, and that is the inevitability of death.

> By virtue of its uniformity, universality and inevitability, death is perhaps the most normal of all physiological states.
>
> *American Medical Journal*
> September 1968

We, however, live in a time-generation that unwittingly denies death. Our quest for indestructible mortal life is so determined that we may find it nearly impossible to conceive of dying. "Everybody has got to die, but I have always believed an exception would be made in my case," said William Saroyan, author of *The Human Comedy,* in the days just prior to his death. And surely many of us would agree. Few of us die of age itself, however. Barring accidents, we all have almost unlimited options for prolonging our lives and dying in accordance with the divine principle of nature. The basic causes leading to death are usually civilization's underdevelopment and overdevelopment, underactivity and overactivity, underindulgence and overindulgence. Today's researchers believe that accident or disease, and not old age, cause death. For example, physical disability and death caused by heart problems have been found to have little to do with normal aging; and changes in cardiac output are most often due to disease, not age. The majority of people are plucked from the "tree of life" before they are really ready for death and before true old age has been achieved.

It is estimated that approximately two out of three deaths and one out of three hospitalizations in the United States are linked to a few key risk factors that are potentially preventable causes of illness and premature death. Advances in health care, sanitation and nutrition have largely been responsible for lengthening the life-span. Much health-status progress comes from major modification in fundamental behavior: in what we eat, how much we engage in healthful activities such as exercise, our ingestion of smoke (direct or passive), our drinking, our drug taking (prescription and non-prescription), and in the quality of environment in which we live.

> Appropriate use of drugs requires sophisticated judgment on training and experience gained in medical education, not on psychology curriculums.
>
> Thomas F. Burks, President,
> American Society for Pharmacology
> and Experimental Therapeutics

Ten times the number of medicinal drugs have been developed in the last twenty years as the previous twenty. While some of these have contributed to increased longevity, how have the astronomical amounts of money spent on drugs and health care improved the status of health for the mature adult? The *AARP News Bulletin*,

(April 1989) reports: "Tens of thousands of older people are living in an 'inhuman and needless' stupor induced by misuse or overuse of prescription drugs. The problem of over-medication and mis-medication is so widespread that some people are calling this the nation's other drug problem." Dr. George Simpson, director of clinical psychopharmacology at the Medical College of Pennsylvania, recently said, "Symptoms blamed on old age are often nothing more than reaction to drugs and medication," and he concluded,

> Up to 29 percent of insanity cases among older people, and the reason for one out of every seven hospital admission, can be charged to the same [drugs and medication]. With drugs, one is always balancing the risks against possible benefits. Drug interaction and over-medication often cause such symptoms of aging as forgetfulness, disorientation, and sensitivity.

Every drug has its unwanted side-effects, even the common aspirin. And the overuse or misuse of drugs accounts for rising numbers of disease- resistant strains. In addition, most physicians receive little training in geriatric medicine or geriatric mental health. While 75 percent of medical schools now have courses in geriatric medicine, less than 10 percent of medical students take them, and less than 2 percent of practicing doctors take continuing courses in geriatric medicine. Gerontology, the branch of science that deals with the special problems of aged persons, only became of interest in the 1950s. In his book *Drugs* (The Body Press), H. Winter Griffith, M.D. writes: "Drugs are poisons. A drug cannot 'cure.' It aids the body's natural defenses to promote recovery. Before anyone decides to take a drug, her or his doctor must ask, will the benefits outweigh the risks?" One-fourth of all drugs in the United States are sold to people over sixty-five. Many drugs cause more problems than they solve. Modern people have been trying to maintain good health in order to live to a so-called ripe old age. To do this we have sometimes doctored and medicated ourselves to the point of total reliance, making medical science our idol and the sole means to longevity. Norman Cousins, the self-healer, believed that his own reluctance to accept the inevitability of death kept him from being "trapped in the cycle of fear, depression and panic that frequently accompanies an incurable illness." Doctors told him he had a rare disease of the connective tissues—a disease for which there was no known cure and which eventually would lead to an excruciatingly painful death. He lived twenty-six years beyond the fatal diagnosis.

> *Drugs are not always necessary.*
> *Belief in recovery always is.*
>
> Anatomy of an Illness
> Norman Cousins

In the past forty years much progress has been made studying the relationship between food intake and the causes of disease. Yet despite advances in technical knowledge, doctors still know less about how to promote good health than how to treat sickness, and improper nourishment remains one of the main threats to good health. It has been estimated that between 15 and 50 percent of all people over the age of 65 in the U.S. are undernourished, and more than half of hospitalized patients may suffer some form of malnutrition. Biologically, the body is the substratum of the mind. No commodity is more valuable, more precious, or more desirable than a healthy mind-body. An unsound physical vehicle is a barrier to graceful maturity, yet some people take better care of their automobiles than of the vehicular forms called bodies.

Of the factors that influence a person's chances of surviving to age 65, the most important are mental outlook and lifestyle. Man's spirit may have been created in heaven, but his body, which is "a temple of the Holy Spirit within you, which you have from God" (1 Cor 6:19 RSV), must be lived in and cared for on earth, and it ill becomes any man or woman to harm or dissipate his or her body. What we do with our bodies, how we care for them, is primarily our responsibility and not that of the doctor, the analyst, a spiritual or religious mediator, our parents, or even God. We alone are the best caretakers of our human bodies, the sensors, the best doctors of what is wrong with us, and the first to benefit from the resolution of the problem. People have aged and died prematurely merely through their mental acceptance of aging. The quality and longevity of life depend not on "father time," but on the health, love and vitality given to life by the consciousness that takes dominion over it and governs it from its very beginning. Youth, maturity, old age, are not different states of consciousness but different concepts of the same consciousness.

> I must say to myself that I ruined myself, and that nobody great or small can be ruined save by his own hand.
>
> Oscar Wilde

The mere extension of life without reasonably good health cannot contribute to happiness. As a volunteer worker for Bide-A-Wee, an adoption home for dogs and cats, kittens and puppies, I and other volunteers have visited the various nursing homes for elderly shut-ins in our vicinity. We would take two or three puppies and kittens for an hour several times a month to the aged as part of their recreational therapy program. I was stunned to find so many residents suffering from the ravages of old age, helpless, confined, wasting away, before their time. Some were praying to die or just waiting to die. Many had no disabling physical handicaps but seemed in bondage to age, having mentally given up on life. Others seemed mere appendages of the machines that sustained their lives, unable to understand or interact in any way with the world around them, prisoners of medical technology. It brought to mind the observation of Hippocrates, that that which is used develops, but that which is not used wastes away. It has been estimated that one out of every four Americans over sixty-five will end up in a nursing home. Today there are 2.5 million elderly citizens in nursing homes, and twenty years from now the estimated figure will reach five million. The average cost of an annual stay in a nursing home on Long Island, New York, is approximately $55,000, and twenty years from now the estimated figure will be $100,000 plus. Are we so absorbed and hypnotized by "this time world," and our minds so preoccupied with survival, that we have no hope, no promise for another way of sustaining life? A healthy body promotes a sense of agelessness. Longevity alone does not. We need to remind ourselves consciously and constantly that the body is not a self-acting instrument, but a temporary inanimate vehicle of conscious awareness. My body is not me, nor is it my true entity; rather it is my human identity. My body is merely the house in which I temporarily dwell. It is a mental structure, a vehicle of collective thoughts, and it is in a constant state of renewal. We (that is, our bodies) are not puppets of destiny, although the body is very much like a puppet; and until we, the puppeteers, manipulate it through mind or consciousness, it remains motionless, inactive, dormant. The piano does not tell the pianist how to play. The automobile cannot tell the driver how to drive. The body cannot tell the mind how to live. Our state of mind has an immediate and direct effect on our physical state and vice versa. When the mind is unconscious, the body is out of control. The body is nothing more than mind or consciousness in action. The key to longevity with quality is, then, the supra-mental consciousness. Without it, human life remains programmed, earthbound, and in bondage.

A Haiku Riddle

I sat on his knee,
I, from a stump of a tree
No depth, no breadth, lifeless.
My mouth opened wide, unconsciously without effort.
My eyes glared, his voice came through:

A Ventriloquist's Dummy

Jess E. Weiss

Calendars have assumed a most important place in the present numerical design of human affairs. What is a calendar date but a recording of the length of time it takes the earth to revolve upon its axis? And what is a calendar year but the time it takes the earth to revolve about the sun? Calendars were made for people, not people for calendars. Years of usefulness, sagacity, health and happiness are not to be measured by the pages of a calendar. Individuals must learn to transcend the tyranny of the calendar. When we know life as eternal, we cease to count our years by the calendar. If we desire perennial youth, we must replace mythical beliefs with the eternal facts of being, where there is no eleventh hour. Perennial youth is found only in eternal life and that is the fruit of knowing God aright.

> Every part of us that is sensitive and alive is spirit; and everything in us, from head to toe, is alive and sensitive. That is why, when the body is separated from the spirit—which is called dying—we are still ourselves, and still alive.
>
> Emanuel Swedenborg
> statesman, philosopher, theologian

Now imagine a world without calendars, where life is not measured by a birth date and a death date. If you did not know how old you were, how old would you feel? When someone dies, no matter at what age, it is commonly said that the demise was "untimely." When is death timely? Timely death, natural death or transition from this finitc body, is time for regeneration, renewal and rebirth, because birth and death are only different processes of earth-bound consciousness. They are the opposite poles of the same lines. In a sense, death of the body begins at the moment of conception. "Life gives birth to death and death gives birth to life—and each is the womb and tomb of the other," says Lao Russell in *God Will Work With You But Not For You* (Walter

Russell Foundation). Birthdays only give credence to the aging process leading to the Old-Testament limitation of three-score and ten. Why is it that obituary columns must state the age of the deceased? Why is it that all tombstones and gravestones record the dates of birth and death? Why are we so fascinated with the ages of those who have died? What's so important about these numbers? Why not use this space to note that he or she passed this way and left a legacy of kindness, gentleness, or compassion? No one expressed this sentiment more succinctly than Henry Drummond when he wrote in his little book, *The Greatest Thing In The World,* "I shall pass through this world but once. Any good thing therefore that I can do, or any kindness that I can show to any human being, let me do it now. Let me not defer it or neglect it, for I shall not pass this way again." We live in deeds, not years, and we should be remembered not for the numbers, but for the divine love expressed during our life-span, however long or short.

When we see an aging, ailing body, we are beholding an erroneous concept of the divine idea. The Greek philosopher Plato was right: "What thou seest, that thou beest." Emanuel Swedenborg said, "The world we live in is the world that we perceive." And the nineteenth-century astronomer-physicist, Samuel Langley, was right also when he said that the color we see is in us and not in the rose. Or, as the late philosopher Joseph Campbell pointed out, the people we admire are a reflection of our inner selves. This is the theory of metaphysics that all color, form and substance originates within the individual. We create our own mental reality, imposing thoughts upon it, interpreting all we see with our personal vision or lack of vision. We embody mental concepts that then become part of our body of thought. The unillumined person who is most age-conscious is often the one who starts aging the earliest, but agelessness can be found in the illuminated consciousness of anyone who intuitively senses eternity as infinite and as the reality of life.

Aging, paradoxically, can become an exercise in overcoming the false beliefs about age. This is accomplished not by seeking the fountain of youth but by living the Eternal Fountain of "Life," by affirming the experience, vision and wisdom of age, by believing in eternal life instead of the illusory changes we behold in this life; by early giving the mind sustained training in overcoming the false habits and beliefs our forefathers have had about age; and by transcending the concept of time, that is, birth, birthday, death-day. In this manner we bring about the perpetual youthful consciousness of spiritual existence, which in turn maintains youthfulness of the body. The body is always the obedient servant of the mind. Consciousness prepares, maintains and sustains the body it knows.

What we see serves as a mirror of our inner selves, which someday we will manifest physically. By the same token, our outward appearance reflects the quality of our inner life and vision. The Hindu religion teaches that when the end of mortal life comes, a person should not hesitate to forsake the body for a more fit and beautiful form, and prepare to awaken where there is no fear, sorrow, hunger, hate, thirst or death. The cardinal Hindu belief is that the body is created out of consciousness. There is an old Taoist adage of a sage who dreamed he was a butterfly and then awoke to find himself wondering who was doing the dreaming.

We experience our dream of aging according to our own designs. "Contemplating life as having no beginning and no ending, and seeing our own lives as existing in timeless being, helps us to escape from the belief that we must some day die" (Carl J. Welz, *The Warm Line*).

> Life can grow with age and reach beyond the fading walls of flesh. Can know that death is but the other side of life.
>
> Emanuel Swedenborg

There is a human desire to escape mortality, physical limitations, and the fetters of time and space. Our invisible God-life is eternally never-changing but our visible sense of mortal life is continuously changing. We need to aspire to know immortality, not in the hereafter, but in the here and now. The hope for immortal life after death is a basic tenet of religions. But belief in immortality now is nondenominational, nonecclesiastical, nonsectarian.

There are many thought forces in "this world" seeking to offset the human sense of ageless being and immortality. The law of averages, nursing homes, the mortality table, funerals, cemeteries, health statistics, the ages at which one's parents die and the causes of their deaths, and the age-old Bible limit of three-score and ten are examples. The common view of aging is of a mortal thinker incarcerated inside a physical body. Scientifically, there is no proof that aging is normal; it is an accepted happening. To change the misconception of growing old, one needs to awaken to the reality of agelessness in eternal life. We innocently enter the world with dignity, and we desire to leave the same way. To know God as Father is to sever the umbilical cord of birth and death. Life is but a moment of eternity.

> *Turn not to the outside world!*
> *Into thine own self go back!*
> *In the inner man alone truth resides.*
> Saint Augustine

> *With God is the fountain of life.*
> Psalm 36:9 KJV

Chapter III

Living and Dying Gracefully

> I BELIEVE in the sacredness of the human body, this transient dwelling place of the living soul, and so I deem it the duty of every man and every woman to keep his or her body beautiful through right thinking and right living.
>
> Elbert Hubbard

Life expectancy was just twenty years in Greek and Roman times. Alexander the Great died at thirty-three, which was at that time (323 B.C.) classified as late middle age. Shortly after the signing of our Constitution in 1790, just 201 years ago, life expectancy in America was thirty-two years, and it remained at that point until 1820, when it began to increase, to 47.3 years at the turn of our century, to approximately sixty-five years in 1947, and then 74.7 years in 1985. By 1988 there were sixty million Americans over fifty years of age. After baby boomers, the 65+ age group was the fastest growing one between 1970 and 1980, and this trend promises to accelerate. Today there are approximately twenty-nine million Americans who are sixty-five or older, or one in every nine Americans. The number of Americans over age sixty-five exceeds the entire population of Canada. It has been estimated that this 65+ age group will reach 35 million by the year 2000, that it is expected to increase to 39 million by the year 2010, and that it may soar to 87 million by 2040. In 1900 there were only 123,000 Americans over 85. Today they number 2.8 million, and by the year 2020 this segment of the population will increase threefold. In the early twenty-first century there could be two million Americans over 90 years of age. In 1988 there were some 54,000 Americans age 100 or over, ten times the number in 1950. The United States National Institute on Aging says that far more Americans will live into their 90s and 100s in the very near future. The Social Security Administration last year published a longevity chart showing that the older we get, the greater our life expectancy. The chart reads like this:

In 1990	Life Expectancy	
Age	Female	Male
25	83.1	76.2
45	82.8	77.3
65	84.9	80.6
85	91.9	90.5

Costly medical advances add years of life for some, but not necessarily years of health, and the bright picture painted by these statistics hides some other, disquieting facts. Statistics also show that the individuals most likely to require long-term health care are those sixty-five and older; that this health care need is expanding at an unprecedented rate, with one out of every four persons in this age category entering a nursing home during his or her lifetime; and that the people most at risk to commit suicide are not the young, but those on the opposite end of the scale. The National Center for

Health Statistics shows that persons over sixty-five represent 12 percent of the U.S. population, but account for nearly 20 percent of all reported suicides. The latter years of life do carry a high risk of self-inflicted death. Further, the financial burden for caring for the disabled elderly is catastrophic. A United Nations-affiliated group called Impact states, "The cost of subsidizing disability in age is probably far greater than the cost of preventing disability." Health-care costs have risen from $75 billion in 1970 to $620 billion anticipated this year (1991), and are expected to soar to $1.5 trillion nationally by the year 2000.

The United States devoted 7.4 percent of its gross national product to health care in 1970, 9.1 percent in 1980, and now pays almost 12 percent, amounting to more than a billion dollars a day, which is more than any other nation in the world pays. And still we do not have the greatest average longevity or the healthiest population. Of the industrialized nations, the U.S. ranks 17th in life expectancy and an appalling 20th in preventing infant mortality. Furthermore, a growing number of health experts argue that the U.S. no longer has the financial resources to provide unlimited medical treatment for all those who need it. The only solution, they say, is to ration health care.

In his new book, *Playing God*, Dr. Thomas Scully says: "For the first time in history, physicians have the ability, know-how and sophisticated technology to sustain the physical life of patients beyond any reasonable quality of life they might want to endure." The mere extension of life without reasonably good health does not automatically contribute to happiness. To many, life support is really death deferral. An anguished physician from Blackfoot, Idaho, whose father also was a doctor, wrote of modern medicine's epidemic of protracted dying: "To my father, premature death was the constant enemy. Fifty years later I have been too successful at stalling death. I have prolonged the act of dying for poor souls whose times, by rights, had come. With the excuse of 'saving lives,' and with a little technology, I have justified tortures worthy of the Inquisition. The relatives of these patients have been twisted to the breaking point by the wonders of modern medicine. Protracted dying is an American epidemic" (*Readers Digest*, December 1987). And this is despite a famous New York Court of Appeals 1914 decision which states: "Every human being of adult years and sound mind has a right to determine what shall be done with his own body." Do you remember that in 1984 the former Colorado Governor Richard Lamm spoke out about the terminally ill's "duty to die and get out of the way"? Today he says: "Medical science and longevity have presented society with a new and often terrible reality. The American way of death is more frightening than death itself. Our bodies are outliving our minds. I fear living in a forgotten corner of a nursing home, drooling and incontinent, my heart beating but my mind dysfunctional. I fear not death, but that under some circumstance I will not die."

Is it any wonder that a legal battle over euthanasia, the painless death, which the Greeks called "an easy death," is looming over our civilized society? The National Hemlock Society, founded in 1980, supports the option of active voluntary euthanasia for the terminally ill. People today do not want longevity alone. We want to be in control, to have something to do with the rules of living and dying, and not be subjected to the scientific practices of others, which can keep us alive in a helpless body by artificial intrusions, or unwittingly intern us for life in a hospital or a nursing home. We want the right to die with dignity, and we do not want to force our families to deal with our "persistent vegetative state." Because of modern medical technologies, the timing of a person's death is often decided by health-care professionals. Many patients are kept alive by unnatural methods after all hope of cure has vanished. Not everyone wants to live when life is not worth living. It is my sincere opinion that life ends the moment a person loses the will to live. Concerning the right to die, a recent poll conducted for the American Medical Association found that 73 percent of the public approves of withdrawing life-support systems from hopelessly ill or from irreversibly comatose patients if they or their families have requested it. Within ten years, possibly five, euthanasia will be a part of good medical care, says the National Hemlock Society, whose key objective is to provide people with the option of dying with dignity. Speaking of dying patients in his inspiring book, *Love, Medicine & Miracles* (New York: Harper & Row, 1987), Dr. Bernie S. Siegel agrees: "In the face of such courage, time and again I've wished I could do something to ease the passage. I feel that my profession's methods of attempting to prolong life and cure disease, among the noblest goals of our civilization, were sometimes crueler than the way of the wild, where serious illness is quickly relieved by death." More leading doctors are writing in medical journals that maintaining the lives of such patients is cruel and that suspending treatment is morally justifiable.

By June 1991, forty-eight states and the District of Columbia had already passed laws specifying the terms under which living wills are considered valid; these allow individuals to demand that they not be kept alive artificially. By the turn of the next century, such statements will be as common as indicating a beneficiary on a life insurance policy. This year New York became the first state to approve legislation that makes it easy for individuals to name a surrogate who would be empowered to make all health-care decisions for the individual—including the decision to withdraw life-support systems should the individual become incapacitated. This involved setting up a panel of experts in health, law, and ethics to develop a comprehensive set of guidelines for deciding when to forego or halt life-sustaining treatment of dying patients. Curtailing such treatment is called DNR, *D*o *N*ot *R*esuscitate. Other states also are seeking passage of laws giving patients the right to establish "living wills" granting "the right to die with dignity." The alternative is to die vegetatively, suspended between life and death while loved ones fight for the patient's freedom from an indeterminate artificial existence. It is right for people to control their health care under all circumstances, even unto death.

Professor Sidney Hook, a teacher of philosophy, has published an essay advocating euthanasia, and in a recent interview he stated:

> Most people say life is sacred and is worth living in all circumstances. I would argue that life is not worth living in all cases. Sometimes the worst thing you can know about a human being is that he survived. My father was stricken with hemiplegia. His speech and motor centers were paralyzed on one side. It took him twenty-two years to die. He practically died by inches. The only prayer I had for him was a prayer for relief of his suffering. At that time, I felt

> that the quality, not length of life, was the important thing. It's no life to live on a mattress-grave somewhere—unable to live, unable to die. I say that acknowledging the right to die is a way of preserving the dignity of life.

To live relatively free of the degenerative processes that presently plague our adult population should be our scientific goal. "To me, more important even than how long a person lives is how well they live," said Dr. Christian Barnard, the renowned heart specialist. Dr. Daniel Callahan, who writes on ethics in medicine, concurs: "I want to argue that medicine should be used not for further extension of the life of the aged, but only for the full achievement of a natural and fitting lifespan and thereafter for the relief of suffering." Scientists today agree that our lifespan potential is about 110 years, although some scientists speculate that we might have the capacity to live to be 130 or 140. In the twenty-first century, the aging process will be slowed through improved nutrition, exercise and preventive medicine. The greatest achievement of this century by medical science is the extension of the lifespan; but without *quality* of life, vitality, mentality, and activity, what good is longevity!

> I've just turned 40. When Mozart was my age, he had been dead five years. Jesus, seven. Martin Luther King Jr., two. I know more than ever before that when it comes to human life, quality matters so much more than quantity. Our goal is not to live forever. It is to live in such a way that when we die our lives will prove to have been worth dying for.
>
> F. Forrester Church,
> a Unitarian minister

Researchers are beginning to unlock some of the mysteries of growing older. Many of the myths, misconceptions and stereotypes associated with aging are being destroyed. The minutest cell belongs to a community of cells, and the greater identity is called the body. Biologists tell us that the body's trillions of highly specialized cells and tissues are constantly being replaced, giving us a built-in system of physical renewal. When the cells are healthy, the organs are healthy; when the organs are well, the whole body is filled with youthful vitality. But if something goes wrong, then the entire body suffers and ages more quickly. The key to both understanding and overcoming the disabilities associated with aging rests with the body's self-protective immune system. Our immune system keeps us alive and healthy, and a properly functioning immune system is a formidable barrier to disease and that aged feeling. Dr. Ronald Lawrence, director of the Western Geriatric Research Institute in California, has stated, "Athletic decline comes not from a chronological number but from smoking, excessive drinking, poor nutritional habits and not exercising on a regular basis." Lawrence, who is sixty-one years old and has completed more than 120 marathons, says that age alone is not a valid reason for feeling stiff or fatigued. He further advised, "As you get older you should be able to do all the things you could at twenty, with only a slight decrease in aerobic capacity and endurance." An article in the *AARP News Bulletin* (September 1987), entitled "How We Age," reported on the findings of gerontologists, scientists and researchers studying the aging process. Their conclusion was that intellectual performance continues throughout one's lifetime, and that physical decline attributed to aging is really due to disuse, and is much more avoidable than previously believed. Most of us have accepted without question that our reactions get slower and slower as the years go by. But scientists who question that belief are finding surprising evidence that age actually slows our reactions very little. Dr. Alexander G. Reeves, chairman of the neurology department at Dartmouth, claims: "We are finding that in normal people, aging is more of a psychological perception than a physiological change... [Generally], eighty-year-olds solve problems just as well as twenty-year-olds, given just a little more time." How we have been programmed! For generations we have been taught that we age because of wear and tear, that we are old by the numbers.

Many of today's mature adults are defying society's stereotypes of "old age." From all appearances they are smarter, healthier and more productive than their predecessors. James E. Birren, retired dean of the Andrus Gerontology Center, University of Southern California, has cited studies of human performances showing that the intellectual capacities of adults have increased from generation to generation. "Put simply," he said, "adults of today know more than their counterparts of several generations ago...and the average college graduate has about half the vocabulary (22,000 words) he or she will have at age sixty-five (45,000 words)." Researcher David A. Waldman of the State University of Binghamton, New York, analyzing the findings of thirteen employment studies done from 1940 to 1983, found that as one gets older, one's productivity increases moderately but steadily. "Too many people place a lot of importance on how aging affects performance, believing older people cannot do jobs as well. Our evidence proves that's not the case," said Waldman. By adjusting our thinking, which in turn affects our behavior, we can live longer and more actively, and not be older and sicker, but older and better.

It is ironic that in the economic world one may be too young to occupy a certain position, and when old enough to qualify for the position, he or she will soon be too old to retain it—and this despite the Federal Age Discrimination in Employment Act of 1967, which makes it unlawful for employers to discriminate because of age and prohibits companies from coercing older workers into accepting early-retirement incentives when they want to continue to work. The traditional retirement age of sixty-five should not apply to this century's adults. The "senior citizen" age label was set by the Social Security Act of 1935, when life expectancy was about sixty. In *An Autobiography* (New York: Bantam Books, 1987), Lee Iacocca writes: "Let's face it: mandatory retirement is a terrible idea. . . In Japan, it's the older guys who are still running things. . .the youngest guy I talked to was seventy-five. Sure working can kill you, but so can not working." Japan is the world's most rapidly aging country, and its population has the largest percentage of aging (over sixty-five) citizens in the world. Forty-six percent of Japanese men sixty-five and over continue to work at jobs, compared with 18 percent of American men. It has been estimated that by the year 2020, one out of every five Japanese will be sixty-five and older.

In his latest book, *Talking Straight* (New York: Bantam Books, 1989), Iacocca says of American attitudes:

> Once upon a time people just got old gracefully. Now, as soon as someone gets on in years, even if

> he's still a vibrant and healthy person, everyone says, Gee, he used to be a great guy, but now he's seventy. What's that supposed to mean? I know plenty of guys who are lethargic at twenty. Because of Hollywood and TV, this country believes in forever youthful, forever young, forever happy. It directly associates happiness with health and beauty. It's no wonder then, that the attitude of most young people is: Sixty is getting old, seventy means decrepit, and eighty means forget it.

A special advertisement section in one of our popular business publications, under the heading, "The Disappearing Quality of the U.S. Work Force," says that American business is starving for qualified workers. Many executives of large corporations are becoming aware of a valuable pool of potential workers—men and women in their sixties and seventies with physical and mental attitudes of people in their prime. Perhaps in the twenty-first century, their ages *will* be considered prime. A successful business needs wisdom as well as energy.

Herbert W. Armstrong, founder of the Worldwide Church of God, died in his sleep a few years ago at the age of ninety-four. Fifteen years ago he said: "I have produced my greatest accomplishment since I hit the calendar age of 80. Of course that's not my actual age; it's only what the calendar says." At the height of his career, age 83, he wrote: "Many corporations have retirement programs timed to age 60 or 65. Somehow I could never quite understand that type of outlook on life. I have never reached 'middle age,' at least not consciously, not in my mind and manner of thinking and acting. I have been too busy to think of 'growing old' or ever retiring."

He proved that one can be a participant in the calendar system, without being its victim. He did not just occupy space, he filled it. Ralph Waldo Emerson said: "The first wealth is health." Health means wholeness. If you are healthy, you are active no matter what your age, and if you are active, you are whole and more likely to be in good health.

On January 1, 1987, Congress passed a landmark civil rights bill to ban mandatory retirement based on age. The law prior to that time could force workers in the private sector to retire at seventy regardless of the valuable, experienced contribution they could make to the economy's work-force. Former President Ronald Reagan, the oldest president in history (seventy-eight), signed the bill, which was sponsored by the late Representative Claude Pepper, the oldest lawmaker in Congress (eighty-eight). Intellectual competence can improve at any age, and the more we use our minds the sharper they will stay. Advancing years is not illegal and therefore not punishable. Calendars were made for people, not people for calendars. Why should one's consciousness age?

If the Roman philosopher Cicero (45-44 B.C.) were asked to comment about today's preconceived ideas about age, his reply would be just as refreshing in this century as it was centuries ago:

> Does old age take all the fun out of life?
> Cicero: "When people complain like that, the fault is one of character not of years."

> Does old age cause memory to fail?
> Cicero: "No doubt it does, if you don't keep it in trim or if you're born a trifle dull."

Does old age deprive us of all pleasure?
Cicero: "The person who sits in the first row of the theater enjoys it more, but the one who sits in the last row still enjoys it."

Does old age diminish strength?
Cicero: "I never liked that proverb. Get an old head early if you want an old head long. There are some invalids who can't participate in life's activities, but such disability isn't peculiar to old age; it is rather the usual concomitant of ill health."

Does old age mean death is near?
Cicero: "What could be more in accord with the Law of Nature than for the old to die? Fruits, if they are green, must be forcefully pulled from the bough, but if they are ripe and mellow, they drop off naturally."

In *The Village Comedy,* Mortimer Collins wrote: "The true way to render age vigorous is to prolong the youth of the mind." A sound mind manifests a sound body. To the degree that we understand this, our limited sense of life dissolves and is replaced by a conscious acceptance of graceful agelessness, of infinite Being. What happens around us and to us affects us, but is not as important as the reaction within us. The way is not easy and "few there be that find it," but it is possible. God inhabits eternity. If we could refrain from measuring and limiting all that is good and beautiful, we might enjoy more than threescore and ten and still maintain our vitality, our youthfulness, freshness, and promise. The mythical, limiting beliefs of age must give way to an understanding of the eternal facts of being. Eternity is not an extension of time—it is a continuation of infinite Being without youth or old age. When we truly believe this, the fetters of finite existence will begin to fade, and the age labels will begin to disappear. But until then, we are compelled to obey health laws and to use medical physical aids for healing. "I will restore to you the years that the locust hath eaten," wrote Joel, the Bible's prophet of revival (Joel 1:4 KJV). So, what are numbers on a birth certificate? Nothing but ink. The secret of qualitative longevity is to die young, late in life.

If I Had My Life To Live Over

> If I had my life to live over, I'd try to make more mistakes next time. I would relax, I would limber up, I would be crazier than I've been on this trip. I know very few things I'd take seriously any more. I would take more chances, I would take more trips, I would scale more mountains, I would swim more rivers, I would watch more sunsets. I would eat more ice cream and fewer beans. I would have more actual troubles and fewer imaginary ones. You see . . . I was one of those people who lived prophylactically and sensibly and sanely, hour after hour and day after day. Oh, I've had my moments and if I had it to do all over again, I'd have many more of them. In fact, I'd try not to have anything else, just moments, one after another, instead of living so many years ahead of my day.
>
> I've been one of those people who never went anywhere without a thermometer, a hot water bottle, a gargle, a raincoat, and a parachute. If I had it to do all over again, I'd travel lighter, much lighter than I have. I would start barefoot earlier in the Spring,

and I'd stay that way later in the Fall. And I would ride more merry-go-rounds, and catch more gold rings, and greet more people, and pick more flowers, and dance more often. If I had it to do all over again. But you see, I don't.

From *The Journal of Humanistic Psychology,*
by an 82-year-old man dying and
accepting death

Chapter IV

New Dimensions

AYURVEDIC, the Hindu "science of life" medicine, the four-thousand-year-old Hindu art of prolonging life, uses transcendental meditation, massage and herbal therapies to trigger the body's natural healing response. Dr. Deepak Chopra, an endocrinologist who has practiced Ayurvedic medicine, poses an intriguing question: "Inside of us there must be a 'thinking body' that responds to the mind's commands.But where could it be, and what is it made of?"

> This perishable nature must put on the imperishable, and this mortal nature must put on immortality. When the perishable puts on imperishable, and the mortal puts on immortality, then shall come to pass the saying that is written: "Death is swallowed up in victory."
>
> 1 Cor 15:53-54 RSV

In the latter part of the nineteenth century, a spiritual renaissance occurred in the Western Hemisphere: the Christ-like healing effect of metaphysics was rediscovered. It reestablished the basic principle that there exists within man a state of consciousness which deals with what is beyond the physical or experiential. This "alternative medicine" treatment for physical and mental ills was the groundwork from which arose the practices of psychiatry, psychology and psychoanalysis. The state of the human mind affects the health of the body. If the receptive human mind would realize and experience a sense of immortality, then to the degree that it did, the illusion of mortality as reality would dissolve. The primary principle of this alternative medicine is that God made man in His own spiritual image and likeness, and this likeness cannot encompass ill health, age and debility. It is not a question of one's faith in religion, but rather in God. Where God is, there is religion and immortality. The search for wisdom is philosophy, the hunger for truth is revelation, the love for God is religion.

Over a century ago Mary Baker Eddy wrote: "Neither the Old nor the New Testament furnishes reasons or examples for the destruction of the human body, but for its restoration to life and health as the scientific proof of 'God with us'. The measurement of life by solar years robs youth and gives ugliness to age." This metaphysical transcendental thinking bears witness to that which is beyond human understanding and inculcates that there is no divine law of death, decay or debility for men and women. It means that human beings of their own free will can leave this man-made aging kingdom and evolve naturally into the God-based, ageless kingdom that is right here, right now.

> As Dr. Michael Zasloff watched a frog swimming in its tank, a flash of insight struck him. The frog had recently received a surgical cut, and the frog's cut was healing nicely and without inflammation despite the bacterial playground in the tank. Why? What did the frog's system possess that allowed it to fight off the harmful bacteria? After months of numerous test and failures, Doctor Zasloff isolated

> two natural antibiotics in the frog's skin that fight off a wide range of bacteria, fungi and parasites. There is evidence that the antibiotics fight even some forms of cancer.
>
> In recent years, Susumu Tonegawa, a Japanese molecular biologist, was awarded the Nobel Prize for Medicine for pioneering research unlocking the mystery of how the body's genes produce billions of different antibodies to fight disease, and how the body's immune cells reshuffle their genetic material to help make antibodies that recognize and attack bacteria and other foreign organisms. Scientists say that, in years to come, research may lead to new treatments for cancer and for autoimmune diseases based on helping the body generate and control antibodies.

Although many might consider the two discoveries mentioned above to be the century's major breakthroughs, I do believe that greater still will be the wider acceptance of the fact that human beings, by changing their inner state of consciousness, can control the outer expression called body. Today there are those in the medical profession who will tell you that nearly all diseases have a psychosomatic component. More people than ever before have the backbone to go against medical tradition and search for alternative approaches to health and well-being. No longer does the old cliché "doctor knows best" necessarily apply. We Americans have been victimized for too long by a kind of medical mystique, which has caused us to perceive our well-being to be totally in the hands of the omnipotent health-care professionals. Old age is a dis-ease, a conscious mistake; a discordant and discomforted concept in the mind of man. It is not God-ordained.

A recent related positive development is the increased recognition of the value of a holistic or wholistic approach to medicine. It is a New-Age philosophy which emphasizes the need to look at the whole person, including emotional, intellectual and spiritual aspects, and not just physical symptoms. It is an increasingly popular form of therapy, and it is fast becoming a basic consideration in all forms of health care. Holistic medicine relates disease to the conscious state of an individual and promotes the idea that by altering the conscious state, the ability to change the physical state is developed correspondingly. It means simply that ultimately we are individually responsible for our own health.

In 1973, Edgar D. Mitchell, Apollo 14 astronaut, founded the Institute of Noetic (Mind) Sciences. Its goal is "to support research and educational programs to expand mankind's understanding of the nature of consciousness and the mind-body link." These researchers are developing evidence that the mind is the key controlling factor in virtually all disease. The researchers call it "healing from within." They contend: "If the mind plays such a major role in the onset of disease, why shouldn't it be possible to use the mind to restore health, or, better yet, to avoid illness altogether?" The limited power of material curative methods is often disappointing, and expensive medical technology is often ineffective. Not every disease responds to medicine and surgery, and therein lie the essential limitations of these methods. In spite of improved methods of early detection and treatment of many diseases and plagues peculiar to modern civilization, disease and disability continue to exact a frightening toll on our society. Medicine and medical technology have not brought us the answers to the problem of aging. Rather than being content with medicine's short-term successes, we must analyze the long-term results of our "progress" and recognize the cumulative social burdens of the aging society we are creating. Medical authorities now believe that over fifty percent of all those seeking medical care are sick or disturbed because of mental problems, fear, tension, worry, anger, or a combination of these or other disharmonies. Doctors are not trained to deal with their patient's emotional disharmonies and frequently are not interested in them. But treating the whole person—body, mind and soul—is often necessary for permanent healing to take place.

The book *Love, Medicine & Miracles* by Bernie S. Siegel, M.D., sheds light on the healing ability of one's consciousness and seeks to inspire the hopelessly ill to want to live, to expect to live, and to find a way out of their physical dilemma. Dr. Siegel gives case after case of individuals who have helped heal themselves of the worst of diseases by changing their mental outlook. This medical pioneer has a new-old approach to treatment. He says: "My role as a surgeon is to buy people time, during which they can heal themselves. I try to help them get well and at the same time to understand why they became sick. Then they can go on to true healing, not merely a reversal of one particular disease." He was putting into practice what Hippocrates taught around 400 B.C., when he said he would rather know what sort of person has a disease than what sort of disease a person has. Albert Schweitzer, the renowned missionary doctor, said, "Each patient carries his own doctor inside him," and Luke, the physician of the Bible, recalled Jesus reading to the members of the synagogue from the book of the prophet Isaiah on the subject of healing, admonishing them, "Physician heal thyself" (4:23 KJV). Norman Cousins' philosophy is that every person must accept a certain measure of responsibility for his own recovery from ill health. He chose to "laugh" himself out of a crippling, terminal disease. As a result of his success, there are today "humor rooms" in hospitals where patients can go to see videotapes of movies with Charlie Chaplin, the Marx Brothers, or Laurel and Hardy. Allen Funt, creator of T.V.'s "Candid Camera," said recently: "Norman Cousins started us on the charitable road of sending selected material to sick people all over the world." Cousins and Funt were only doing what Aristotle prescribed over 2,000 years ago when he described the habit of laughter as "a bodily exercise precious to health."

One doctor tells about a cancer patient who was advised by her physician that all she could do now was "hope and pray." When she altered the course of her disease and was questioned about how she accomplished her healing, she replied that her doctor prescribed the only medication that could cure her, and he never knew it. The body knows only what the mind dictates. Medical professionals have put so much stock in drugs that they tend to forget the potential power of the body's immune system and the spiritual avenue of the mind which governs that system.

> *Give me the serenity to accept*
> *the things that I cannot change,*
> *the courage to change the things*
> *that I can, and the wisdom to know*
> *the difference.*
>
> The Serenity Prayer

The reader might well ask, "Are you suggesting that mortals could live forever?" Of course not. But I see no reason why people in the near future cannot leave this human existence discounting age, without a debilitating and dehumanizing death struggle, for whatever is beyond mortality. I believe all of us yearn to illuminate our own understanding of what we are about as human beings; we are driven by the desire to know why we are here, why we die, and what is after here. What most people do not realize is that it is not natural for the body, God's holy temple, to be sick. God gave us our bodies, and we have misused them. That, and that alone, is the cause of all our suffering. God did not create a sick, aging, debilitating image; nor did God prescribe the finite life limit of three score and ten accompanied by physical and mental deterioration. Our simple acceptance of the fact of our creation in His "image and likeness" is curative medicine. A human being is the conscious image and likeness of God, who owes fidelity not to a finite limited law but to an unlimited infinite law. Illness and the ailments of old age are not the will of God but rather the effects of our separateness from God's will and grace. Old age is a man-made belief, a human projection. If a person can turn from the mesmeric programming and the negative conditioning about age and the aging process, the foundation for quality of life with longevity is laid. When we feel "old," life is not worth living; we are preparing to die.

Myself when young did eagerly frequent
Doctor and Saint and heard great argument
About it and about: but evermore
Came out by the same door as in I went.

Omar Khayyam

So long as individuals attempt to achieve eternal and ageless life by means of the human mind alone, like the Persian poet Omar Khayyam, they will come out the same door as in they went.

We human beings have three resources for healing: medicine, mental belief, and spiritual understanding. Despite decades of tremendous advances in medical knowledge promoting health and longevity, it will take the exercise and intervention of individual and universal God-realization to make this diseased, age-obsessed world whole. Medical doctors help people to live longer, but they do not know how to keep them vitally active and in good health, particularly in their later years. The disciple and physician Luke of the Bible tells us of the woman who hemorrhaged for twelve years and had spent all her wealth on doctors in her search for healing. Finally she was healed by her own Christ-like receptivity merely by reaching out and touching the hem of Jesus' garment (Luke 8:43-48 KJV). Medical science has its limitations; God, the divine healer of all life "Who forgiveth all thine iniquities and who healeth all thy diseases" (Psalms 103:3 KJV), has none.

> *Lord, Thou canst heal me because*
> *Thou dost control the life, atoms,*
> *and subtle conditions of the body*
> *that doctors cannot reach with medicine.*
>
> Man's Eternal Quest,
> by Paramahansa Yogananda,
> Los Angeles:
> Self-Realization Fellowship, 1975

Part II

Deep within us all
There is an inner sanctuary of the soul
A hidden place
A divine center
To which we may continually go.

Here is the slumbering God
Awaiting to be awakened
And be our life.

Thomas R. Kelly
A New Testament Of Devotion

Chapter V

Sharing the Journey

IN BUDDHISM, a *bodhisattva* is one who has encountered the divine, but who chooses to return to the world of appearances and help others rather than to enter nirvana. We all are called to encounter the divine and become divine helpers of other human beings.

1. A Friend in Need

In the early fifties, my life took a complete turn. In 1954, I began working for the Aetna Casualty & Surety Insurance Company as a Workman's Compensation claims examiner reviewing work-related accidents. I was still recovering from World War II, which had left me seriously handicapped both physically and mentally. Nine years after receiving a service-connected medical discharge, I was still a foxhole agnostic struggling desperately to understand the truth of being. The religious concept of God as omnipresent and omnipotent clashed with the reality of the war and the postwar period. "Is God in the likeness of man or is man in the likeness of God?" Belief battled disbelief. Then in 1956 I became interested in a metaphysical approach to health and in a new way of life, the open door to greater works promised by men of the Bible. My agnosticism, my multiple war disabilities, the medical aspects of my insurance work, and my new-found understanding warred within me, compelling me to spend almost every lunch hour in a nearby library studying the Bible and inspirational literature. I felt a great need to find out more about that "kingdom within" and the fundamental truth of creation. I lost my agnosticism and became a theist, a believer who accepts God's existence and earthly influence. I began to awaken to the belief in an Omnipresent Deity who, when properly realized, answers. The following personal experiences are some of the reasons why the substance of my faith went beyond the evidence of things seen.

In the second or third year of my new-found understanding, my company's supervisor, in recognition of my ability at work, presented me with a large new corporate account for a heavy-machinery equipment company that had its own nursing staff in case of emergent accidents. The head nurse of the corporation, Lillian, called me daily and reported all work-related accidents for immediate adjudication and timely Workman's Compensation payments. Lillian would call me right after my lunch study hour in the library, and I would advise her of the proper procedure for filing each accident claim. We always talked longer because I had come fresh from my inspirational Bible reading, and my thoughts and my thinking were temporarily free of personal stress and self-absorbed problems; and she too felt my sense of comfort and peace of mind. Soon we became "spiritual buddies" via the telephone, even though I was Christian and she was Jewish. We both began to look forward to these daily calls, for after she gave me her report, we would continue our metaphysical discourse on our relationship to a supreme Creator. Her responsiveness and receptivity to this transformed state of thinking was so great, that our discussions became inspiring and uplifting daily occurrences for both of us. This went on for six or seven years.

One late evening while at home, I received an urgent telephone call from a doctor affiliated with a hospital in the Bronx, New York City. A patient in the hospital wished to see me immediately. It was my telephone friend Lillian, whom I had never met personally. The doctor told me that she was in the intensive-care unit, was dying, and had requested my presence. At first, I felt totally inadequate; the demand seemed, at that moment, too great for my level of understanding. The mere thought of attempting to help another in such a dire state seemed premature. But a voice within said: "The root of the tree of life is eternal life. Practice what you have preached and be consciously, not piously, one with Me. You are My transparent image and likeness through which *I* perform and perfect that which *I* give you to do."

In a few moments I was in my car. When I got to my destination, I was in such deep meditation that I did not realize how I had gotten there or that I had even arrived. At first, hospital personnel did not want to let me in because I was not related to the patient, merely an acquaintance. Besides, visiting hours were long over. I simply requested that they at least tell her I had come, and that I was downstairs. The next moment I found myself by her bedside. As a new student of metaphysics, I found the setting I encountered totally alien to every comfortable spiritual God-like concept with which I had aligned myself. Tubes, intravenous devices, doctors and nurses were everywhere, and my friend was heavily sedated. I did not know at the time that she was lying on a bedpan. I leaned over and closely whispered into her ear that God's message and messenger was here. She nodded slightly; her eyes were closed. Then the following message came through me as I *listened* spellbound: "*Nothing* can prevent the sun from rising in the East and setting in the West. *Nothing* can prevent the moon and the stars from appearing at night, and *nothing* can prevent the earth from rotating on its axis." At that very moment Lillian gave out a horrifying death-defying scream that scared the living hell out of me, and I was requested to leave the hospital at once. Two weeks later she was discharged from the hospital. She wrote:

> Jess, my doctor told me that my appendix had burst and peritonitis was rampant, and I was slowly dying of bodily poisoning. My pores had closed and for some time I was not eliminating or excreting the proper waste material from my body, so they had me on a bedpan. Whatever you said to me opened all the eliminating channels and filled the bedpan, and that is what made me scream so. My doctor called it a miracle. How can I ever thank you for coming to this medical nurse, a stranger dying in a hospital, who is not of your faith—and bringing me yours.

2. The Good Neighbor

Several years later, I went to work as an independent life insurance agent for the Travelers Insurance Company. In the beginning, while I attempted to build a clientele, I found myself with much time on my hands. For inspiration and courage to face a day with nowhere to go and no one to see, I would turn to the Bible for guidance. On this particular morning the Bible lesson for the day was Jesus' parable of the Good Samaritan: There was a man traveling the road from Jerusalem to Jericho, who fell into the hands of thieves who robbed him, beat him, and left him half dead. A priest going down the same road saw him, but passed him by on the other side. A Levite came on the scene, and when the Levite saw him, he too passed by. Finally a Samaritan traveler came along and took pity at the sight of him, bandaged his wounds, and brought him on his mule to an inn. He paid for his lodging and care until he was well again.

On this summer morning I was driving aimlessly, when something made me turn down an unfamiliar side street. Out of the corner of my eye I observed a man who had just fallen on the sidewalk. But I kept going. I have enough problems without getting involved, I thought. Then the story of the Good Samaritan came flashing before me in full view. To live in a Godlike manner I must hear God's calling, respond to the calling, and be faithful to that calling. I put the car in reverse, and within seconds I rushed to the man's side. He lay in a pool of blood, his face was bluish, and his body appeared stiff. I was convinced he was dying. I took my light jacket and placed it under his head; I leaned over and whispered in his ear, "Speak to me." When I got no response, I placed my lips as close to his ear as I could, and I commanded him to say "God." No response. I raised the tenor of my voice and again demanded he say "God." The white of his eyes rolled back and he moved his eyelids. "Say God," I repeated. "G. . .G. . ." he gurgled. "Not good enough," I shouted, "Say God. Think God." Softly and slowly he muttered "G. . .G. . .G. . .G. . .

God." "Louder," I said, "I can't hear you." "God-God-God," he cried, as if coming out of a deep trance. In a few seconds he was on his feet, and the police and ambulance appeared on the scene at that very instant. They ignored me. I retrieved my jacket, got into my car, and with glory in my heart went about my business. I never inquired who he was or the nature of his problem. I just knew all was well, because I, on that day, had listened to God's voice within, and this was my Father's business.

> Can you see yourselves as spiritual beings having a human experience, rather than human beings who may be having a spiritual experience?
>
> Dr. Wayne W. Dyer
> *You'll See It When You Believe It*

3. The Picture

When my children were growing up and were of Sunday-school age, we became friends with an elderly single woman who lived alone in a small, modest apartment on the west side of Manhattan in New York City.

Theresa Nagle was a Sunday-school teacher and a metaphysicist who wrote inspirational articles for publication. Our children were captivated by her, as I soon became, because of her nonsectarian way of reasoning with us about her concept of God, our relationship with Him, and how He governs our lives if we let Him. She persistently taught that, if you desire to know Him, you must work to understand Him. It is your task, not His; God already knows you.

At least one Sunday a month, we (as many other parents with their children, we later learned) would spend a private and fruitful afternoon in her apartment, seeking through her our own feelings about God and attempting to put this understanding into practice in our own lives. She personally taught me about the philosophy of spiritual being and convinced me that we all have but one true desire, which is to discover, or to rediscover, the missing link, which she said was direct intercommunication with God the Father. For many years I expressed God exoterically until I began to recognize my own concept as merely vicarious philosophy and theology. I realized how limited and stereotyped my understanding had been, and how hungry I was for this new enlightened vision. Soon after, I began crying out to a God I loved, longing to hear: "You have not chosen *Me,* but *I* have chosen you . . ."

Our social-religious friendship went on for many years, and I enjoyed the privilege of sharing scriptural truth with this remarkable spiritual woman.

There hung in her narrow hallway a century-old battered and tattered picture in a shabby old mahogany frame. For years, every time I walked through this hall, I felt drawn to this mystical picture. I felt the artist's inner vision communicating itself to me and to me alone, but I was unable at that time in my life to comprehend its meaning. For many years, I was mesmerized by the picture, but I never understood why, until one day I received a letter from an attorney telling me that our dear friend had passed on and that he was the executor of her small estate. He wrote that she left nothing of real value, but she had wanted all "her student children" to have something to remember her by. She had requested that I perform her funeral service and give the sermon. The attorney requested us to come and bring our children that following Sunday afternoon.

When we arrived we saw literally hundreds of items all over the apartment, all named and clearly tagged for her young friends. When everyone had received his or her inheritance and all items were claimed, we prepared to leave. But "where is the picture?" I wondered. "Who got that?" I responded to my inner prompting and asked the attorney, who had crossed off all of the items and names on his list. Then he suddenly remembered that he had tucked it away in the closet. He said: "Strange that you should ask me for this item, of all the hundreds of items, because this particular item was not mentioned in the will." He said, his face glowing: "I would presume this has your name on it and was meant for you."

I hung the picture on my bedroom wall and subliminally it continued to reveal to me a sense of being at One with the universe.

Several years later, friends undertook to have the picture anodized and reframed for me. When the framer removed the picture, a tattered, age-worn, and almost illegible piece of parchment fell to the floor. It was the artist's handwritten interpretation of the meaning of his work. He called it *Omnipresence* (A full-color reproduction of the picture is on the front cover of this book.):

> Here is a picture which expresses a great and wonderful idea. It is a symbolic portrayal of the spiritual evolution of mankind.
>
> It visualizes the steps in the growth of the world's central aspiration, as it has persistently reached out to find God and to solve the problem of Being.
>
> On the left is blind belief stooped and bent, yet still struggling to rise. For men from the lowest beginning have felt the stirring of God within. His hand

is slightly lifted from the earth in his attempt to separate himself from the power of the material law that seems to keep him down.

In the center stands faith. He is standing nearly erect, yet his head is still bowed. The impassable mountain which rises in front of belief has been removed by faith. Yet because his eyes are still looking down upon the earth, he does not see that the path before him is free and clear.

At the right stands understanding, throbbing with consciousness of full life whose infinite possibilities spread out unobstructed before him. He is facing God and not the earth. The difference between him and faith is essentially one of spiritual vision.

Chapter VI

Of Time and Eternity

I am satisfied with the mystery of the eternity of life.
Albert Einstein

IT WAS EINSTEIN who theorized that a person completing a long journey at close to the speed of light would find, upon returning to earth, that he had aged considerably less than those left behind. If we could travel close to the speed of light, say to a point six light years from earth, the entire trip would take about sixteen years as measured by ordinary time clocks carried aboard our spaceship. But when we returned, we would find that some thousands of years of earth time had elapsed. Time (yesterday, today and tomorrow) and space (here and there) are forms of intuition, merely conditions of human experience.

> Never record ages. Chronological data are no part of the vast forever. Time-tables of birth and death are so many conspiracies against manhood and womanhood. Life is eternal. We should find this out, and begin the demonstration thereof.
>
> Mary Baker Eddy

We can comprehend an hour, a century, even a millennium; but how difficult to grasp eternity! Eternity is without beginning or ending, always present, always existing, without past or future. It is infancy without maturity or old age, and it is always today, never yesterday. Human life is a mere parenthesis in eternity! We have nothing familiar to relate to the infinite or to the eternal. Time has nothing to do with eternity. Time has no independent existence, but is simply a continous succession of temporal events as perceived by human consciousness. Consciousness is not in a brain, and it can exist without the body; but the body cannot function without consciousness.

In the absence of consciousness the human body is a finite, non-intelligent and temporary piece of earthbound, time-bound, space-fettered inanimate matter. It has no sight, no sensation, no feelings. It is spiritless. It knows no birth date, no death date, and no age. It has no consciousness of good or evil, perfection or imperfection, health or sickness, youth or age, and it has no awareness of growth, maturity or decay. It contemplates neither life nor death. The only difference between a living body and a dead body is the presence of an active principle called consciousness. According to Hindu philosophy, the body is always dead. It is the consciousness of mind which energizes and gives the body life form. Without consciousness the secular body decomposes. It is not really Father Time, a birth date, or the calendar that ages us. It is the unseen operator, the labeler, the human mind with its acceptance of time and time's measurement as absolute reality. There is nothing theological about the irrevocable past of the calendar or the unpredictability of its future! It is a mental projection of human statistics, a man-created system of reckoning and recording time. Forever, from the human standpoint, is limited to the time on earth.

Forever Is
But A Moment Aware.
How Foolish To Think
Eternity Is Numbered.
Chan Sei Ghow

We cannot deny the passage of days, but we can consciously reject the tyranny of the calendar. Even the passage of time, which brings that which we call advancing years, is not actually a law that is binding on humanity. Acceptance of this as law is a form of individual malpractice. The body lives and matures through the substance of thought emanating from the flow of consciousness. Physical life (body) is not something separate and apart from one's consciousness (mind). The physical temporary form is merely the externalized yet subjective state of the human mind. Therefore, a change in thought about the body results in a change in the condition of the body, for the body and the human mind are one thing. Consciousness can transcend many physical difficulties when it takes dominion and imparts to the body thoughts of wholeness, completeness, continuity, and purity. It is achieved, not through statements of truth about age, but rather through a state of consciousness that knows the truth of Eternal life. To begin, one must honor one's body through conscious acceptance (physically, mentally and spiritually) of all that is good. The Good Book tells us: "Whatsoever things are true, whatsoever things are honest, whatsoever things are just, whatsoever things are pure, whatsoever things are lovely, whatsoever things are of good report; if there be any virtue, and if there be any praise, think on these things" (Phil 4:8 KJV). When we fail to abide by these principles, death out of season is inevitable. But when we know life as eternal, we can cease to count our years by the calendar and enjoy the timelessness and the fullness of life no matter what the birth certificate records.

Age is an invisible birthmark, a label limiting and handicapping people at every turn. Who determines and defines the age you are? You do! Today's physicians are beginning to realize that "old age" is a disease and has nothing to do with years. Like many other diseases, it is psychosomatic in origin. Fear thoughts, worry thoughts, pain thoughts, aging thoughts: these are the underlying currents which eventually lead to death thoughts and create the ugliness called "old age." Birth and death are on the opposite sides of the same coin. Eliminate the belief in one and the fear of the other, and you have overcome the aging process.

The three constituents of age are the past (youth), the present (maturity), and the future (old age), and these constitute the transitional phases in the continuity of human life. We cannot bring back the past, nor can we live in the future. But we can live in the present totally enlightened. The only human time that actually exists is the present. To fail to live the present time as the only time, that is, "the now," is to lose it. A wise metaphysician explained it this way: There were three men crucified on the cross: Jesus in the center with a thief on each side. One thief represents the past and the other the future; and the son of God in the center is the present, God's image and likeness, the individual, infinite, earthly, Christlike God-idea.

To God there is no past, present or future; all time is *now* at any moment. Concern for the past and the future robs mankind of the fullness and joy of the Eternal nowness of life. The individual who attempts by degrees to live wholly in the present, rarely dwelling in the past, the rearview mirror, and trusting the future, is a person of wisdom. The later, wiser portion of life is perhaps even more important than the earlier because it prepares us for what we will be at the beginning of the next life's experience. For me, I can know that *now* is the first day of my life, and tomorrow is merely the extension of the eternity of now. There is no yesterday, today or tomorrow in *now* because *now* was, is, and always will be. Ecclesiastes taught: "Whatever is, it has already been; whatever is to be, already is," (3:15; James Moffatt, *The Bible: A New Translation*). The awakened and activated nowness of Spirit, the within Christ, will heal and nullify age and ultimately the fear of death. Heaven is oneness with God—Eternal life; hell is earthly separation from God. And the difference between is measured by the degree that we fear death and dying. God's existence may not be understood, but God's presence cannot be denied. Humanity is the visible evidence that there is a God. Man without God is a nonentity. It is said that Eternal-God created man in time and space; if so, man created in earthly time and space will, in due season, step out of time and space into Eternity. There is no death in God and no God in death. God inhabits eternity and I, God's image and likeness, also abide and dwell in eternity. Therefore, I am *in* this time world, but by Grace I am not *of* this time world.

There is nothing sacred about time. People need only to live life as it is, accept it as it is, and not measure it by years and finite standards. Infinite being knows nothing of time. Life is a matter of progress and not profit, a process of self-discovery, and the self-expression of the selfless life within. As Paul writes to the Corinthians:

> *Though the outward man perish,*
> *the inward man is renewed day by day.*
> 2 Cor 4:16 KJV

Ecclesiastes proclaimed, "To everything there is a season. . . a time to be born and a time to die." Death out of season is a mistake. When mortal death comes in its own time, we will see it as a dream, nothing more. It is a freeing of the consciousness from confinement in a physical form.

> Time is no part of the divine life. One who appears to die appeares to have lived in time. Erase the concept of time, and there is no death.
> Carl J. Welz, *The Warm Line*

There is no divine law of death or decay for man, and a theistic understanding of the continuity of eternal life has no sense of time. It is ageless. Earth-life is merely a moment in eternity, and we want our transitory life to be absorbed into the life that is eternal. Belief in eternal life is faith searching for understanding. Says Paul (2 Cor 5:1 KJV): "We know that if our earthly house of this tabernacle were dissolved, we have a building of God, a house not made with hands, eternal in the heavens."

The body's "I want" sense of existence obscures the "I have" realization that life is eternal. The human body is the substance of matter until we understand that it is actually God's spiritual temple. Man is God-imaged, Christ-like. The law of Christ (Grace) predates, predominates, and dissolves the *quid pro quo* law of karma. The body is one's temporary experience; it is not one's entity, but merely one's human identity.

> Since these [spiritual] forms or substances are not visible to the physical eye, people today have only the notion that insights and thoughts are abstract things. This is the source of the insanity of our century, that people do not believe they have a spirit within them that is going to live after their physical death, when in fact this [spirit] is a much more real substance than the material substance of their body.
>
> Emanuel Swedenborg

"If a man dies, shall he live again? This thought gives me hope," cried Job. Our present mortal bodily state is merely the vestibule for the realization that within us is always something evolving, something substantial, something vital, something wonderfully lifelike that is destined to live beyond the body's short span of temporary physical life. If the body is not our essence, then what is? Consciousness is! Consciousness does not just exist; it is Existence. The secret of life is consciousness. We live in a visible world of bodies and an invisible universe of consciousness. Until this is acknowledged, even if imperfectly, our greatest anguish will continue to be how and when we consent to give up this temporal form, imperfectly seen as body. Lao-tzu, founder of Taoism, expressed it perfectly about 600 B.C. when he wrote:

I suffer when I believe
That the body I have is me.
With the body not me
Would my suffering still be?

Cecile B. DeMille enjoyed getting off by himself to reason out a problem. One day, while just drifting quietly in his canoe on a lake in Maine, he drifted close to shore where the water was just a few inches deep. Glancing down, he observed that the bottom was crowded with water beetles. As he studied their maneuvers, one of the beetles came to the surface, slowly crawled up the side of the canoe to the top, and, grabbing fast to the wood, died.

Hours later, he noticed the beetle again and saw that its shell had become dry and brittle from the hot sun. As he watched, it split open and, emerging from the dehydrated shell, came a new form, a dragonfly. The dragonfly without hesitation took to the air out of the old husk. Its scintillating colors dancing in the sunlight, it winged the waters with a rebirth and a challenge. In a moment this new winged insect flew farther than the water beetle had crawled during its entire lifetime. As the dragonfly circled back and swooped down to the surface of the water, it hovered over its original birthplace, casting its shadow on the water. Perhaps the water beetles who were its friends and relatives below observed it too, but they showed no recognition or comprehension of it, and the atmosphere above them remained a world unknown and incomprehensible. They were still living in their limited beetle state of conscious existence, while their winged counterpart had found unlimited freedom, with the earth and sky as its heavenly abode.

When DeMille related this fascinating experience later, he reasoned: "Would the great Creator of our universe do that for a water beetle and not for a human being?"

We live in time so little time
And we learn all so painfully,
That we may spare this hour's term
To practice for Eternity.

Robert Penn Warren

Chapter VII

The Promise and the Fulfillment

The Old Testament was the question,
the New Testament the answer.
The Old Testament was the problem,
the New Testament the solution.
The Old Testament was the promise,
the New Testament the fulfillment.
Jess E. Weiss

THERE ARE two separate and dissimilar biblical accounts of creation in Genesis, the first book of Moses. The first and earliest document was written about 900 B.C. and the second about 500 B.C., both by unknown authors. The two contradict one another in theology and philosophy as well as detail, and they reflect radically different ideas about creation and the nature of man and his relationship with God. The seeds of our genesis, our heritage, our mortality and immortality, cause and effect, and life and death are found here.

The Old Testament account of the Adam creation dates from long after the time of Moses; he never taught the Hebrews such a theory. In the first Hebrew account, the one Moses knew, God (Elohim) created; in the second, the Lord-God (Yahweh) formed. The name Yahweh (meaning 'to be'), later changed to Jehovah, came into use five to seven centuries after the time of Abraham and Isaac. In the Elohistic version of Genesis, man was created last and in the divine likeness; in the Yahwistic account, the earthy mortal man was formed first "of the dust of the ground," and the Lord-God had to breathe "into his [Adam's] nostrils the breath of life." Some consider this narrative of Adam an allegory; others look upon it as a literal account. The renowned Christian theologian and mystic Thomas Aquinas (1225-1274) had a theological explanation for what he called "The Genesis Myth":

> Man and woman created in the state of original justice lived happily in Paradise in harmony with themselves, harmony with one another, and harmony with God. But by sin they were cruelly divided, split, scattered. Beguiled by the serpent, expelled from Eden, ashamed of their nakedness, they fell into that sadly divided state to which their children are now reduced.

In this century, the 1982 *New Encyclopedia Britannica*, reports: "Up to modern times the Jewish and Christian believers generally accepted this [the Adam concept of creation] as a historical account of human origins; but the science associated with the new hypothesis of evolution cast serious doubts on the historical character of the narrative. Biblical scholars now recognize that the writers of Genesis were not trying to write a natural history but to express their beliefs concerning the relationship of man with the universe and with God the Creator. The composition is properly called a myth of origins, 'myth' meaning expression of basic truth."

About 100 B.C. Philo, a Greek philosopher and Hebrew theologian, had an ingenious theory. He taught the concept of two original Adams: one heavenly, the other earthly. The heavenly Adam man, he said, "is the scriptural first man who was made in the image and likeness of God; he is imperishable, an idea perceptible only by the intellect." The earthly Adam man, "as we see him now in the races of the world, is imperfect and corruptible." Man's genealogical heritage seems to be a biological and spiritual enigma. Even the disciples of Jesus differed in their concept of his human birthright. Matthew traces the human lineage of Jesus from Abraham with no mention of Adam. Luke begins Jesus' genealogy twenty generations before Abraham, all the way back to Enos, to Seth, and to Adam. Jesus himself says:

> Have you not read that He which
> made them at the beginning
> made them male and female.
>
> Matthew 19:4; Mark 10:6 KJV

Jesus never recognized or referred to the Adam concept of creation, nor did his disciples. In the Book of Revelation, which was composed about 96 A.D. and is the only book of prophecy of the New Testament, St. John, Jesus' most beloved disciple, made no reference to the Adam theory of creation. It was the apostle Paul (at one time an Old-Testament zealous pharisaical rabbi), who made the separation between the earthly and heavenly man. Paul frequently preached that the first form to inherit the earth was Adam, and he was the first to refer to the "fallen man's" mind (Adam mind concept of man) as "carnal," having "enmity against God." The earthly Adam is identified with the fall of man and stands figuratively for original sin and death. In the first account, all was the creative work of God, including the creation of male and female, which are but two aspects of the nature of God in human persons. In the second, Yahweh shared with Adam the process of creation and surgically removed the rib of Adam to make Eve. The first verse of Genesis, "In the beginning God created the heavens and the earth," is the very first statement in the Bible, and it confirms God's word that He was from the beginning of the world, and that He is the origin of each and everything. It reveals God as Cosmic consciousness, Christ consciousness without form, who created infinite, eternal and immortal man and woman in His own image.

This God from the beginning is not God only of the beginning, but God for all eternity, the Alpha and Omega. And this eternal deity gave mankind "dominion . . .over every living thing" and life without end. And the Divine-Creator finished His work and saw it as "very good." Where, then, is the necessity for recreation or procreation?

In the Book of Genesis, *second* chapter, sometimes called the Adamic Covenant, the laws of physics are imposed, and Adam and Eve are presented as the progenitors of the human race. Two of their offspring, Cain and Abel, reflect, respectively, the mortal and the spiritual aspects of human nature. Cain, the firstborn earthling, slew his brother Abel out of jealousy, because Abel's offering was more pleasing to Yahweh than his. The second chapter tells us that that which is conceived in sin and brought forth in iniquity is condemned to die. God has become an anthropomorphic Lord-God: knowing evil as well as good; possessing human attributes, passions, and manlike characteristics; punishing and rewarding, giving and withholding. That second chapter of Genesis depicts, not God's creation, but the author's mistaken concept of a celestial Creator. Adam and Eve, according to this second chapter, were given a choice by a Lord God of how to live their lives. They could choose the immortal tree of eternal life—or the mortal tree of death. They ignored their creator's advice, and through their sin chose to live in a dual world of good and evil, cause and effect, life and death, with an anthropomorphic deity and a finite human existence, with a Lord God in heaven and man on earth. Man dies, not because of Adam's sin, but because universally man believes that he is a descendant of the first man God supposedly created. Writing in *The City of God*, St. Augustine gave this view:

> The first men were so created, that if they had not sinned, they would not have experienced any kind of death; but that, having become sinners, they were so punished with death, that whatsoever sprang from their stock should also be punished with the same death.

Why must men and women be subjected to the beliefs of their forefathers? As Jeremiah 31:29 (*The Living Bible*), puts it: "Children pay for their father's sins." This is the curse of Eden: "But there went up a mist from the earth," writes the author of the second chapter of Genesis. The mist of misconception and deception has obscured the grandeur of divine reality from the beginning. Nowhere in the Old Testament is man identified or referred to as "the son of God."

I would rather be in hell with God
than in heaven without Him.

Meister Eckhart
13th-century German mystic

In the Old Testament man attempts to use God. In the New Testament he serves Him. The Old Testament is dying but has not yet died, and The New Testament is coming to birth but has not yet been born. According to the Old Testament, "God in man" was called Elohim; in the New Testament, "God in man" is the Christ. Around 60 A.D., Paul wrote to the Galations: "Thou art no more a servant, but a Son; and if a Son, then an heir of God, through Christ." The monotheistic zeal of the Hebrews for one Lord-God, Yahweh or Jehovah, however, so eclipsed the Elohim-God doctrine that it is practically eradicated from the Old Testament. God said to Moses: "I appeared unto Abraham, unto Isaac, and unto Jacob, by the name of God Almighty, but by my name Jehovah [or Yahweh] was I *not* known to them" (Exodus 6:2-3 KJV). When Moses returned from communing with God on Mount Sinai, he found the Israelites worshipping a molten calf. Their concept of God was so limited by their tribal, personal, Jehovistic sense that they forsook the "image and likeness" Creator, turning instead to something objective and external to worship, an inanimate idol. Unfortunately, the Elohim deity, the "God with us," the "God within," the "tree of life" and "image and likeness" doctrine, even today has been largely superseded by belief in a tribal personal Lord-God Jehovah and represented by the tree of the knowledge of both good and evil, cause and effect, young and old, life and death.

The apostle Paul taught that all men die by virtue of their descent from Adam: "Since by man [Adam] came death, by man [Jesus] came also redemption and the resurrection of the dead" (1 Cor 15:21 KJV). "If you belong to Christ, then you are Abraham's descendants and heirs of the blessing God promised" (Gal 3:29 Beck). The Bible tells us that God created man in His image and likeness; therefore, whatever He is, we are. It is the Adam man who undertakes to make an image of God. By identifying with the Adam creation we have "put on the old man" and the imperfections, beliefs and limitations of Adam. Our divine heritage is forgotten, and we believe primarily in our Adamite human inheritance. But Jesus tells us (John 8:51):

> *With all earnestness I have to*
> *tell you this—no one who obeys*
> *me shall ever die!*
>
> *The Living Bible*

When Robert, age 9, was told by his Sunday-school teacher that he had every right to question God on the subject of creation, he wrote: "Dear God, Do you consider Adam your son or is he like an invention? Which is it?" I believe that it is not the entombed Christ but the risen (the awakened) Christ in us that dissolves the Genesis myth, that breaks the fetters binding us to the Adam dream. The Adam man in the course of biblical history has changed the "image and likeness" creation beyond recognition—from God who created humankind in His own image and likeness, knowing only a divine beginning without end, to a Lord-God and a man beguiled. "As was the man of dust, so are those of dust, and as is the man of heaven, so are those who are of heaven" (1 Cor 15:48 RSV). The divine birthright as God's image and likeness pre-dates the introduction of Adam and Eve, yet most religionists have chosen to embrace the latter concept of creation, almost to the exclusion of the other. Humanlike, changeable and unpredictable is the Deity of the second chapter of Genesis. We must reevaluate the concept of the Garden of Eden before Adam and Eve. "In the beginning was the Word" (John 1:1 KJV), the Divine truth. As *The Living Bible* phrased it: "Before anything else existed, there was Christ, with God." Jesus said, "Truly, truly I tell you, I [the Christ nature—the Light] have existed before Abraham was born" (John 8:58 Moffatt). God-imaged humanity can see and know that the real "kingdom" is not without, but within themselves from the beginning. When we truly know this, we can stop asking "Where is God?" The mystical poet Tennyson put it simply: "God is closer than breathing, nearer than hands and feet." A moment without God is a moment without a sense of life.

God is Creator and man His creation.
God is Light and man His shadow,
And in Him is no darkness.

Jess E. Weiss

Ezekiel, the prophet of hope, revealed: "You were perfect in all you did from the day you were created until that time when wrong was found in you," (8:15 *The Living Bible*). Adam has been described as the first "god" of Hebrew mythology. From this mythological standpoint, the one god and creator entered what he created and then disappeared in the atheism of Adam mortality. This mortal experience, Adam's polytheistic experience, having many gods, many rituals, and many idols, is a dream. Only God-realization enables man to distinguish between the real and the unreal. Human life is a journey from physical cognizance of the body to spiritual awareness of the mind, from a mortal sense of finite existence to an immortal realization of infinite Being.

> Entirely separate from the belief and dream of material living is the Life divine, revealing spiritual understanding and the consciousness of man's dominion over the whole earth.
>
> Mary Baker Eddy

We are like a man who dreamed that he was being chased by a ferocious lion. As he was about to be devoured by the lion, he ran into a solid brick wall. Having no alternative, he decided to pray; then he turned and boldly faced the lion. When the lion was just a few feet in front of him he stared into the lion's mouth and in a state of panic cried: "My God, my God, what do I do now?" And the lion replied: "I don't know, this is your dream." In dreams, things are only what the dreamer makes them be. When Jesus was told that his friend Lazarus had been dead and in the grave four days, he said he would awaken him out of the deep sleep. When Jesus went up into a mountain to pray, he talked with Moses and Elias, men who had been dead for centuries. The apostle Paul, who wrote more books of the Bible than any other author, said he saw and spoke with Jesus after his death, resurrection, and ascension. To fulfill the promise of spiritual and eternal life, we must be awakened out of the false sense that human experience is divine reality, for the only reality is eternal God-life.

Lead me from the unreal to the Real
Lead me from darkness to Light
Lead me from death to immortality.
The Upanishads

On June 6th, 1944, on Omaha Beach, where I was awarded the Bronze Star Medal, a foxhole buddy severely reprimanded me saying, "Jess, you *tell* me there is a God—now *show* me there's a God, and I'll believe it." If only I knew then what I know now, that you have to believe in something before you can know it. Our illusion of finite mortality began with Adam and Eve. It should have ended when Jesus was resurrected, and our understanding of immortality should have awakened when Jesus ascended. "Where mortal self ends, God begins," said Meister Eckhart. Jesus proved for us that men and women are not their bodies; rather, they *have* bodies. Our state of consciousness, that is, those thoughts we allow to govern our bodies, determines our "fountain of life," our longevity and its quality. God-Life and God-Consciousness cannot be entombed in a body.

To believe in the Resurrection and Ascension rather than in the ingrained concept of death is the key. The Bible regards death as an "enemy" to be destroyed. The invalidation of the mortal aging state invites us into the vestibule for immortal ageless growth. Is the death of the body, young or old, the finality of being? For this question the world begs an answer. Human life continues because it has a single purpose, which is to find Eternal life—God. Eternal life is not something we may hope for after death, but something we are engaged in here and now. We are eternal entities bound by the earth-weight of our bodies and the closing-in walls of time and space until all sense of mortality is spiritually dissolved from our consciousness. For surely we are never *in* a body; nor does the body *have* a spirit. Rather His eternal image and likeness has a form. Human beings need a body for consciousness in time and space; they have a heavenly form for consciousness in eternity. Hindu scriptures teach that birth and death are manifestations of *maya* ("that which is not"), cosmic delusion, and that the incarnating ego may require a million years to obtain liberation from the illusory sense of life in a body. Birth and death have meaning only in the Adam world of mortality. They represent a rendering "unto Caesar the things that are Caesar's." There is no record that Adam ever awakened from the dream of mortality. "All are of the dust and all turn to dust again," wrote the unillumined and fatalistic preacher of the Bible, Ecclesiastes. Dust is nothingness, and consciousness never becomes dust. No atheist has ever proved that we die into nothingness. It seems more reasonable to me that, when I die, I will not die into a sense of nothingness but return home to the Omnipresence of Allness.

> *The fool hath said in his heart,*
> *there is no God [No Truth].*
> Psalm 14:1 KJV

The karmic (Adamic) law of birth and death duality is the cause and effect of quid pro quo: something born, something must die; the Yin and Yang, the positive and the negative, the action and reaction—which are all good and evil concepts of the Garden-of-Eden philosophy of that second chapter of Genesis that I discussed earlier.

> Seventy years are given us! And some may live to eighty. But even the best of these years are often emptiness and pain.
>
> Psalm 90:10 *The Living Bible, Old Law* theology

> I am come that they might have life, and that they might have it more abundantly. And whosoever liveth and believeth in me shall never die.
>
> John 10:10; 11:26 KJV, *New Grace* theology

The mythical belief by which we limit life, strength, and wisdom to three-score and ten revolutions of the earth around the sun is a decoy and a prison sentence to everyone who believes it. Our human frailty, fallibility and frustration engender in us a necessity to believe in God-Eternal life. "If God didn't exist," Voltaire said, "men would find it necessary to invent Him." Men and women are created in God's eternal image, but without a sense of eternity we shorten our lifeline, and death becomes reality.

The Bible teaches us that God *is* our Father, that He *is* infinite, without beginning or ending, and that we *are* His infinite offspring. The infinite cannot be circumscribed by anything finite; therefore God the Father is ageless. Are we, His infinite offspring and God's idea of Himself, not also ageless, eternal and infinite? Is the ephemeral, material sense of existence reality, or is it simply a misconception of reality? Was Saint Paul correct when he counselled his flock to "put off the old man. . . .and put on the new man" (Col 3:9-10)? "Do you not know that you are God's temple [body] and. . .that God's temple is sacred, and that is what you are?" (1 Cor 3:16 Moffatt). The body is a temple of truth, and like a house of worship, it reflects the truth it reveres. Faith and understanding must form a bridge between time and eternity.

A twentieth-century mystic, Joel Goldsmith, reminded himself daily:

> My body has neither qualities nor quantities of good or of evil. It has neither sickness nor health, is neither large nor small, has neither life nor death: my body is the temple of God. It is God-substance expressed as form, embodying and including all the qualities and quantities which constitute God, the I AM, the Soul. My body has neither youth nor age: It is as ancient as God and as young as each new day. My body is governed neither by laws of matter nor of mind, but by the Grace of God. God is the light of my body. In my body is neither material darkness nor mental ignorance, for God is the Light unto His holy temple, which my body is. God unfolds, discloses and reveals Himself as body, as temple, a place of holiness and peace. God's grace maintains and sustains His body, which my body is. As for birthday wishes, I shall just wish that you didn't have any birthdays so that you could get used to the idea of the continuity of conscious existence without a break or a stop. This is a vision of life without beginning and with no ending.
>
> *The Art of Spiritual Healing*

God does not work for you but through you, provided you release the imprisoned Christ splendor. Oh, to know what is the truth, to know God aright and to reason aright! That *is* life eternal. This mystic knew that a birthdate is as unreal as a deathdate; the outer eye of the mind is but the vestibule for the inner *I* of eternal consciousness. The age I inwardly express is the age that comes back to me. Meister Eckhart wrote, "My soul is as young as the day it was created."

I am youthful; I am youth.
I am healthy; I am health.
I am strong; I am strength.
I am immortal; I am immortality.
A yogi's affirmation

It is a person's imperative duty to keep his or her body in good condition in order to enable the mind to concentrate on devotion and inspiration. To be old, to feel old, is a sin that transgresses God's gift of eternality. One needs to think better of such feelings and be disposed to change and to mature in grace. The one who recognizes and realizes a spiritual and eternal birthright instead of a human, finite, Old Testament allotment of three-score and ten, can live a birthless, ageless and deathless sense of life, that is, an infinite life. Knowing the truth of eternal life "puts on the new man." It robs the grave of victory and "puts off the old man" and the delusion of a lifetime limit.

What we know, we feel, be it old or young. Through thinking and knowing we mold our bodies into a mentally constructed image. To know eternal, ageless life, one needs to know continuously that as God's descendant one is neither sinner nor saint, neither imperfect nor perfect, neither old nor young, never born and never dying; for whatever God is, we are, because God the Father and we, His sons and daughters, are one. "Beloved, now are we the sons of God," said John the apostle, the author of the fourth gospel, who also declared:

"All things were made by Him; and without Him was not any thing made that was made." Such knowledge annuls the curse of Eden and dissolves thoughts of growing older, for underlying these is the thought of the grave. The nature of a finite body is to change and age. The nature of an infinite body makes it changeless and ageless. It is our human nature to grow, mature and die. This material body decomposes, and the gross materials return to the elements. As the second chapter of the Genesis creation says, "Dust thou art, and unto dust thou shalt return," because man and woman, in belief, chose the tree of the knowledge of good and evil, not "the tree of life." But it is our divine nature from the beginning, according to the first chapter of Genesis, in which God saw "everything that He had made," and that "it was very good," that makes our kinship to Him the same yesterday, today, and forever. This is our spiritual birthright, our fountain of infinite eternal youth, our secret to qualitative longevity and to dying young, late in life. The apostle Paul taught humility by "dying daily" to the personal "I," the little self-concept of mortality as reality, and by being reborn in immortality, the greater self. To "die daily" is the self-surrender, by degrees, of a conscious human sense of an aging self to the divine awareness of the ageless self within. I know now that *God is*. Oh God, clear away the dust of my illusory birth and remove my acceptance of a moral sense of creation as reality.

Love lies in this,
not in our love for God
but in His love for us.
1 John 4:10 Moffatt

The beloved apostle John gave us a prescription for longevity with quality when he wrote, "Abide in me, and I in you" (John 15:4 KJV). I now know that the only experience that is real, the only experience that brings happiness, the only freedom from the body, is an awareness of the conscious omnipresence of God within and the accompanying realization of a sense of life that knows no death. Evangelical religion is nothing else but desiring to know God and to be like Him. When men and women begin to search after God, that is evidence that God has found them. The one searching for God searches for everything. And the one who finds God has found everything. "Out of one thousand, one seeks Me; out of one thousand that seek Me, one knows Me" (*Bhagavad-Gita,* often called the Hindu Bible).

Truth is within ourselves.
There is an inmost center in us all,
Where the Truth abides in fullness; and to know
Rather consists in opening out a way
Whence the imprisoned splendor may escape
Than in effecting entry for a light
Supposed to be without.

Robert Browning

Life After Death

Though our bodies are dying, our inner strength in the Lord is growing every day. For we know that when this tent we live in now is taken down—when we die and leave these bodies—we will have wonderful new bodies in heaven, homes that will be ours forevermore, made for us by God himself, and not by human hands. Now we look forward with confidence to our heavenly bodies, realizing that every moment we spend in these earthly bodies is time spent away from our eternal home in heaven. We know these things are true by believing, not by seeing. And we are not afraid to die, but quite content to die, for then we will be at home with the Lord.

Paul
2 Cor 4:16 & 5:1, 6-8
The Living Bible, paraphrased

Chapter VIII

Beyond Human Longevity: A Spiritual Understanding of Age

THE PURPOSE of the human experience is to find the evolutionary portal to eternal life and eventually to embrace and experience God in His eternity, here and hereafter. It is the degree of one's desire to know and to live eternal life which determines one's sense of the infinite birthright of agelessness. The belief of mortality must yield to the understanding of immortality.

> I have come to feel that the whole human story, with all its tragedy and its triumphs, is like a page torn from the middle of a book, without beginning or end—an undecipherable page when cut out of its context. The context of man is the Power greater than man. The human adventure is part of a universal sonnet—one line in a deathless poem.
>
> Joshua Loth Liebman

It is important that we unequivocally reject the ageist concept that all there is to human life is birth, age, maturity, decay and death. Old age is objective. Eternal life is subjective. Life is not a theory of existence, but rather a divine reality with no beginning and no ending.

In his Letter to the Hebrews, Paul wrote that we are made "not after the law of a carnal commandment, but after the power of an endless life" (7:16 KJV). Certainly this applies to the human being whom God created in His own image. This divine likeness, in a human form, is not a mere finite entity with a breath of momentary life, sentenced to live an infinitesimal period of time and then grow old and feeble and disintegrate into dust. Is God so cruel as to put us in a material body doomed to inevitable decay? Death was not part of Deity's original plan when He created His image and likeness. Why do we become so entangled with the world in time and have no time to think about eternity?

> For God made not death, neither has He pleasure in the destruction of the living. For He created all things that they might have their being, and the generations of the world were helpful and their is no poison of destruction in them nor the kingdom of death upon the earth.
>
> *The Wisdom of Solomon* (1:13-14)

Practicing the presence of a God-life with diligence and persistence, one begins to live in the conscious awareness of the immortality of life, and of being *in* a body but not *of* it. "Cease ye from man [the Adam man], whose breath is in his nostrils," says the Book of Isaiah. We accomplish this through acknowledging that a God-life consciousness animates the body and that the transitory body and its brain do not constitute life. We accomplish it through understanding that the entire design of the body and all its processes are governed and controlled by thought. Once this is accomplished, we will be able to "dematerialize" the body in consciousness and to that degree free ourselves from a belief in aging mortality. The "cradle to the grave" concept dissolves, for what we know we then experience. This does not relegate the human sense of life to a realm of abstraction, but awakens it out of the finite and temporary dream-state so that it begins to "have dominion" and "live and move" and have its conscious Being in a sense of eternity. Benjamin Franklin, looking back on life at the age of seventy-nine, reasoned: "I cannot suspect the annihilation of souls, or believe that God will suffer the daily waste of millions of minds ready made that now exist, and put Himself to the continual trouble of making new ones." And he concluded: "Finding myself to exist in the world, I believe I shall, in some shape or other, always exist; and, with all the inconveniences human life is liable to, I shall not object to a new edition of mine, hoping, however, that the mistakes of the last may be corrected."

Unless something greater than ourselves can revive us from the belief and fear of death, we have no hope beyond the grave. A sense of immortal life, of not conforming to this world, is gained not through acceptance of the finality of death, but by a progressive purification and spiritualization of thought while in the living earthly body. When all is said and done, the Father idea, a universal-parent, is still the highest human concept of God.

Man's prayer should be
Not my arms around Thee
But Thine around me.

Jess E. Weiss

Humanly we pray, metaphysically we treat, and mystically we realize the truth. Prayer is not so much our talking to God as it is God talking with us. In prayer we temporarily take off our earthly garment and stand naked, in the abyss of silence, shameless and contrite before our Creator. We turn from an altered human sense to an awakened spiritual consciousness of life. In serene humility we surrender this mortal concept of life, and we become one with Him. In the stillness and dark solitude, we commune with the Light within, in which "God is light, and in Him is no darkness [mortality] at all" (1 John 1:5 KJV). I pray, "Why should I, His image and likeness, be controlled by these human principles?" The mistakes in mathematics, or in scholastic theology, by others, are not my mistakes. I must see through the Adamic archaic theology that treats of God, His personal attributes, and His relationship to me and mankind. Truly, there is no "age" in God and no God in "age." Such prayer is a technique of detachment and a method of gaining freedom from lure of worldly thoughts and the daily routine of a secular, monotonous, material life. It is an avenue of approach to the self-realization that all there actually is to life is a God-life. Prayer is a divine tool for making over that-which-seems-to-be into that-which-ought-to-be.It enables us to know that God exists everywhere He is realized. Soul is the architect, mind is the spiritual builder, and body is the spiritual temple. And man has God-given dominion over his body through cosmic consciousness.

We suffer primarily because of our close identification and idolization of the body. We are not obligated to bow down to this material sense of body-life. The apostle Paul explained it this way: "While we are at home in the body, we are absent from the Lord" (2 Cor 5:6 KJV). By identifying with the body, we have taken on its imperfections and limitations. Both bondage and freedom are products of the mind. If we were a human body only, the loss of that body would indeed end our identity. But we are not this human transitory form, and it is not our permanent residence. We live beyond the limited boundaries of the human form, which can only be here today and gone tomorrow.

> *He who knows the whole world*
> *As the body of his being,*
> *Has dominion over it.*
>
> Lao-tzu

This is mysticism, the universal doctrine that it is possible to achieve communion with God through contemplation and a high state of exalted consciousness, without benefit of outside aid and human reasoning but rather transcending it. It is a sense of being at one with God. Mystical contemplation is the talking of one's soul within Oneself. Mystical experience is the spiritual content of true religion. It is nondenominational and universally available. A mystic is one who has spiritual experiences, hearing God speak through him or her. Moses heard the cosmic voice that spoke out of the burning bush; Saul-Paul experienced it on the road to Damascus. Moses, the servant of God, is called the lawgiver, but innately he was a mystic; so were Paul and all of the prophets. But in this calling, Jesus the Son of God had no equal. The esoteric religious philosophers look on mysticism as the very heart of authoritative religious experience. They see the great prophets as mystics in action, because they were able to see God in His infinite creation. Mysticism is the vocation, religion the avocation, of letting the "imprisoned splendor" of the Christ-nature come through one's humanness so that earth can get a taste of heaven. It is an individual's awakening process of recognizing his or her infinite creation within, even if it takes an eternity. "I AM" is God, without beginning, end, or age and I, as the child of I AM; one who appears as human flesh, am also birthless, ageless and endless. "And the Word was made [appeared as] flesh," said the beloved disciple John.

The prophets and mystics through the ages speak and unveil the truth: man is essentially a spirit, not entombed in a finite human form, but an eternal, infinite, living soul. All scriptures declare a man or woman to be not simply a corruptible body, but a living soul. Years do not make one grow old if one grows in the grace of I AM. Identify with that I AM, that divine Self within, and the body becomes the living temple for the omnipresence of God on earth. This is accomplished when one understands that God is the primary reason for existing and realizes that the only way one can find God is by feeling Him in the self and seeing Him in creation. We need to acknowledge that we have direct access to God with or without a mediator. We need to intuitively feel that I AM is not in a human body; my body is in my spiritual cosmic consciousness which is untouched by human theory and human hypotheses and by the cause and effect of the things of "this world."

> *I may forget* WHO *I am,*
> WHERE *I am,* WHAT *I am,*
> *But*
> *I cannot forget I* AM.
>
> Darwin Gross
> *The Power of Awareness*

When that I-am consciousness reflects a sense of eternal life, then a person's God-life can be neither lengthened nor shortened, thereby demonstrating the dominion of mind over body, and of spirit over mind. We can dissolve a human sense of mortality and enter into a spiritual consciousness of immortality here and now, overcoming the belief of death as finality. One does not have to live in terms of death or impending death; one can begin now to live in terms of the life that is God-life. Nothing really limits us and keeps us in a state of limited mortality but our own thoughts. We should be continually renewing our state of consciousness in accordance with the transcendental truth of immortality. Then the pattern for the renewing process of the body would be such that a more perfect and vital body would result. The physical form is a prototype of the ways in which we are consciously aligned or corporeally misaligned with our incorporeal Creator. God dwells where man lets Him in. Human bodies are given to us, not to be idolized but idealized. The terrestrial body identified with human age is earth-bound; the spiritual idea of body identified with the soul is fetterless and free. The only goal of life is God-realization; only when we comprehend that can our eternal nature assert itself.

> *Except the Lord build the house*
> *they labour in vain that build it.*
> Psalm 127:1 KJV

A consciousness of oldness degrades the life-force that governs the body. An unsound physical body is a hindrance to a sense of agelessness. The soul of man is ever free; it is deathless because it is birthless and bodiless. Birth and death embrace the philosophy of life in time.